THE SUPER EASY AIR FRYER COOKBOOK

THE *Super Easy* AIR FRYER COOKBOOK

Crave-Worthy Recipes for Healthier Fried Favorites

Brandi Crawford

PHOTOGRAPHY BY HÉLÈNE DUJARDIN

ROCKRIDGE PRESS

Designer: Merideth Harte
Editor: Salwa Jabado
Production Editor: Andrew Yackira
Photography © Hélène Dujardin
Author Photo: Jeneé Osterheldt, Lifestyle and Culture Columnist
Brandi illustration by Merideth Harte

ISBN: Print 978-1-64152-049-2 | eBook 978-1-64152-050-8

*To my mother, Denise, my biggest supporter, and Kiya, the best assistant **Stay Snatched** will ever have*

CONTENTS

INTRODUCTION

GROWING UP, WE ATE A LOT OF FRIED FOOD IN MY HOUSEHOLD.
From fried chicken to smothered pork chops to catfish, we pretty much fried *every-thing*. My favorite has always been a big, juicy burger and a side of French fries (I love fries so much I often order a large). Throughout adolescence, I was always labeled skinny, so I didn't worry about what I ate, but those days caught up with me in adulthood. I started to pack on weight, and everyday tasks, like walking up a flight of stairs, became a struggle. This was my wake-up call to focus on my health. I took charge and researched fitness and nutrition, reading everything I could get my hands on. I developed a routine based on advanced weekly meal prep and regular exercise, and my health improved. When I committed to this lifestyle, fried food became a thing of the past.

Enter the air fryer. This seemingly magical appliance has allowed me to reintroduce my beloved childhood favorites because it dramatically cuts the fat. I can now indulge in my fried-food cravings using only a fraction of the oil used for deep-frying.

I admit, the first time I used my air fryer I was nervous—and a little skeptical. I did not fully understand how this appliance could fry food. Naturally, fries were the first thing I tested in my air fryer. I used my simple, oven-baked recipe, monitoring the fries closely to determine when they were finished and how much time had elapsed. I was amazed by the results! The fries were crispy and crunchy, but more importantly, the process felt painless. Next, I tested air-fried chicken wings. Each time I opened the air fryer basket throughout the cooking process, I could hear the sizzle of the chicken. It not only sounded like fried chicken; it *tasted* like fried chicken!

Like any kitchen appliance, it takes time to get accustomed to using the air fryer. As you practice, you will develop techniques that work best for you. One of the first things I discovered is how important it is not to overfill the air fryer. Not only will your food cook unevenly, but it won't have the signature crunch you're seeking. This means some meals may have to be prepared in batches. (Note: I recommend setting food aside as it is finished cooking. Once you have cooked all of your batches, you can reheat the food in the air fryer for a couple of minutes so that the food is warm when served.) I'm eager to share more techniques and processes that have worked well for me on my air fryer journey. Experiments have been my best teacher.

I understand how hard it can be to get food on the table when you're juggling items on a to-do list that's a mile long. The recipes in this book are designed to be easy meals that require only a few ingredients, the majority of which are everyday staples. I've also included substitutions throughout so you can use what's on hand in your fridge or pantry. The air fryer has been very beneficial for my lifestyle because, between workouts and recipe development, I am extremely busy. Many of the recipes found in these pages can be prepared in 30 minutes or less from start to finish. This cookbook delivers healthier everyday meals without compromising the amazing fried flavor we all crave.

Let's dive in!

Chocolate Donuts, page 150

Fried Chicken and Waffles, page 35

CHAPTER 1

Have Your Fries and Eat Them, Too

In this chapter, I'll cover everything you need to start cooking fast and easy meals in your air fryer. I'll outline how air frying works and why this appliance will quickly become one of your most valued kitchen tools. Getting started may seem daunting, but I promise, once you get going, using an air fryer will feel like second nature. I'll also break down the attributes for various air fryer brands currently on the market. My hope is that this information proves to be helpful for those of you in the market for purchase; and if you already own one, you may discover new features of your air fryer you never knew existed.

Easy as 1, 2, 3

With the air fryer, meals in minutes can be your new reality. You will save time making these recipes because there is no need to wait for your air fryer to preheat. For the majority of models, once you power on the appliance, the air fryer heats up instantly. Even the cleanup process is a cinch! Most models include a dishwasher-safe air fryer basket and drip pan (be sure to check out the manual included with your model). Deep-frying can be dangerous, with hot oil splattering, and requires a large amount of oil. It is always a hassle to determine the best way to dispose of the rancid leftover grease. The air fryer eliminates these issues altogether.

My cooking focuses on well-known family favorites and what I like to call "down-home cooking," and that's what you'll find in this book. Main ingredients are easy to locate at your grocery store or consist of staples you already have in your pantry. You don't need to be an accomplished chef to master these recipes. Each is a breeze to create and does not compromise at all on taste. Just be sure to keep your spice rack well stocked; simple seasonings help amplify flavors. I think you'll agree that most of these recipes are perfect for weeknight dinners!

Why Air-Fry?

I love my air fryer for so many reasons: Health, ease, speed, and cost-effectiveness of meal prep top my list. Making this appliance a staple in my kitchen means I enjoy healthy meals in minutes. And it allows me to revisit favorite fried foods that were previously off-limits. If you have been considering cooking with an air fryer, here are the benefits you can expect it to deliver.

IT'S BETTER FOR YOUR HEALTH

Deep-fried foods are loaded with fat and calories, and have also been linked to serious health conditions, including type 2 diabetes and heart disease. Air frying cuts up to 80% of the fat of traditional frying, making it a much healthier alternative. Most deep-fried recipes require 2 to 3 cups of oil. With the air fryer, you need only a tablespoon. Because air-fried meals are so much lighter, you will feel less bogged down after eating them. When I eat a standard burger with fries, I am usually ready for a nap—I quickly feel the effects of excess grease in my body. My experience is much different with air-frying.

EASY CLEANUP

I still have memories of the metal coffee can that sat on our kitchen counter when I was growing up. There was no coffee in the can; the actual coffee was properly placed in the cupboard. This coffee can was filled with leftover frying grease. We never poured our used cooking oil down the drain; we reused it several times before disposing of it. We would throw away the whole coffee can in double-wrapped trash bags, in case it leaked. Traditional frying left oil splatters on the stove, countertops, and even the cabinet above the stove—it was always a hassle to clean up. You don't have to worry about any of that with air-frying. When you finish using your air fryer, there is no excess grease to clean up or discard. Because the air fryer uses nonstick material, simply hand-wash the drip pan and basket or pop your accessories into the dishwasher.

QUICK MEALS

If you are constantly on the go and do not have a ton of time to spend cooking, an air fryer is perfect for you. Most baked dishes can be prepared in an air fryer in a fraction of the time they would take in a traditional oven. Baking and deep-frying require preheating: Before you use an oven to bake, you have to set the dial and wait. With deep-frying, you can't add the food until the oil comes to temperature. An air fryer starts to cook immediately; there is no waiting.

HOW DOES AIR-FRYING WORK?

People ask me this question all the time. I realize it can be quite puzzling to grasp how a kitchen appliance can produce crunchy, fried foods with little to no oil. Here's a peek behind the curtain: An air fryer circulates hot air around the food using a mechanical fan moving at a rapid speed. The heat is circulated very close to the food, allowing the heated air to flow constantly through the food. This yields fast cooking times and crunchy meals.

YES, YOU CAN AIR-FRY THAT

There are so many things you can prepare using an air fryer—this kitchen gadget can do a lot more than just fry. In addition to frying, you can bake, roast, and grill. I fell in love with the air fryer because of its increased functionality. In fact, I find I rarely use my stove these days because the air fryer can pretty much do it all.

Baking in the air fryer will save time and electricity. During the summer months, it will also rescue you from the excess heat of using the oven. One of the most surprising things you can prepare using the air fryer is dessert: from cakes, to donuts, to muffins, to brownies ... Yes, you can air-fry all of that!

Because the air fryer has the ability to act as an oven, you can roast such foods as nuts, vegetables, chicken, and more. The direct heat contact makes the air fryer an amazing appliance for roasting.

Next up is grilling! Using an air fryer grill pan, you can whip up grilled steaks, fish, and vegetables. The air fryer locks in amazing flavor and delivers the perfect texture.

Here are some other examples of things you can prepare:

- Toast
- Bacon
- Cinnamon rolls
- Biscuits
- Grilled sandwiches
- Pizza
- Steamed vegetables
- Corn on the cob
- Baked potatoes
- Fried rice
- Casseroles
- Meatballs
- Pork ribs
- Fajitas
- Salmon and other fish
- S'mores

EASY TO USE

Operating an air fryer is very easy. You merely place your food in the air fryer basket, spritz it with oil, then adjust the temperature and time to cook. There aren't any complex terms to learn and memorize. The process is very simple.

COST-EFFECTIVE

Your air fryer has the ability to fry, bake, roast, and grill. That is an amazing set of features for one kitchen appliance. Coupled with the time-saving benefits, the air fryer will definitely make your life easier for a reasonable cost. Air fryer prices usually start around $100 and range up to a few hundred dollars. You can find air fryers online or at major retailers and department stores.

ENJOY ALL YOUR FAVORITE MEALS

French fries are back on the table! With simple modifications, you can enjoy the same great foods that you have grown to love but were told not to eat. If you are committed to a healthy lifestyle, owning an air fryer opens the door to a world of tasty meal options.

Air Fryer Models

The air fryer market is rapidly expanding, with many brands offering their variation of this appliance. In order to determine which air fryer model is best for you, you need to evaluate your individual needs. Air fryers vary in size, features, and accessories that are included. If you have a larger family, you may opt to purchase a larger model. This will help limit the number of batches necessary to prepare some meals. If you have a small counter area in the kitchen where you would like to store your air fryer between uses, consider a standard 2- to 3-quart size. The air fryers that are 4 quarts or larger will require more space—about the same amount as a toaster oven.

I have two air fryers. When I first heard about the air fryer I became very intrigued. I wanted to see what the fuss was about, but I did not want to invest a ton of money, just in case the purchase didn't work out. I went with the Black+Decker Puri-fry 2L Air Fryer. This air fryer was a great, budget-friendly option to get me going. It does not have a digital dial or any preset, programmable options. It has a knob for temperature and cook time selection.

Once I felt confident in my air-frying abilities, I upgraded to the Power AirFryer. I had heard many great things about that brand, so I did some research and read a ton of online reviews. It has a digital panel with seven preset, programmable options. Preset options make it easy to gauge how much cook time is needed for commonly prepared foods when you do not have a recipe on hand. In just a few touches of the dial, you are on to cooking. I love the look and feel of this model. It's very quiet and crisps food perfectly!

When making the decision on which model will work best for you, you may consider a number of different factors. If you plan to use accessories with the air fryer, then a brand that includes accessories with purchase may be a great option. You may also want to consider the temperature range and maximum allotted time for the preset timer. The timer on some models may go up to only 30 minutes, which can be inconvenient if you are preparing a 40-minute recipe. Some air fryer models do not have an adjustable temperature gauge. You will have to compensate for this by carefully planning how much time cook time should be allotted. An air fryer with adjustable temperature settings is more convenient and versatile.

MODEL	SIZE	PROGRAMMABLE BUTTONS	INCLUDED ACCESSORIES	TEMPERATURE RANGE	TIMER
GOWISE	3.7 or 5.8 quarts	Yes	None	175°F to 400°F	30 minutes
NUWAVE BRIO	3 or 6 quarts	Yes	Grill pan Baking pot Cupcake liners Carrying case	100°F to 390°F	2 hours
PHILLIPS AIRFRYER XL	2.65 pounds	Yes	None	180°F to 390°F	60 minutes
POWER AIRFRYER	3.4 or 5.3 quarts	Yes	Baking insert Pizza pan Cooking tongs	180°F to 400°F	60 minutes
T-FAL ACTIFRY	2.2 pounds	No	None	338°F (only one setting)	99 minutes

Homemade Cherry Breakfast Tarts, page 32

CHAPTER 2

Ready, Set, Air-Fry

In this chapter you'll learn about stocking your pantry with staples that will help streamline your cooking and transform it into a quick and easy process. When I purchased my air fryer, one of the first things I noticed is how easy it was to get started by using ingredients I already had on hand in my kitchen. I will also lay out my air-frying best practices and discuss troubleshooting.

Getting Your Kitchen Ready

You already have your air fryer . . . now what? Let's get your kitchen ready for all the fun. A well-stocked pantry saves you even more time in air fryer cooking. When you have ingredients on hand, the process goes a lot smoother.

SUPER SIMPLE TOOLS

▷ **Cooking spray bottle:** For a lot of recipes, you will need to spritz oil over the food prior to cooking.

▷ **Sealable plastic bags:** Sealable bags work great for seasoning meats. Place the meat and spices in the bag, seal, and shake.

SUPER SIMPLE STAPLES

▷ **Extra-virgin olive oil:** You will need cooking oil for most recipes. Using a small amount of oil will keep the food from drying out and will make the food crunchy.

▷ **All-purpose flour:** Breaded recipes require a flour coating. For gluten-free recipes, coconut or almond flour can be used.

▷ **Bread crumbs:** Seasoned or plain bread crumbs work well.

▷ **Cornstarch:** Cornstarch provides a crispy coating for meat and vegetables.

▷ **Eggs:** Eggs are used for some of the breakfasts included in this cookbook. Eggs are also essential for dredging to help flour, cornstarch, or bread crumbs adhere in breaded recipes.

▷ **Egg whites:** Egg whites have fewer calories and fat than whole eggs and can be used as a substitute. For some breaded recipes, egg whites are used for dredging.

▷ **Cheese:** I recommend purchasing block cheese from the deli or the dairy case and grating it yourself as it melts better than bagged, preshredded cheese.

▷ **Butter:** Use salted or unsalted, depending on your preference.

▷ **Garlic:** I recommend using fresh garlic, but minced garlic in a jar can be used in a pinch as well.

▷ **Soy sauce:** I use this for my Asian-inspired recipes.

- *Salt:* Use iodized, kosher, or sea salt, depending on your preference. Keep in mind that kosher salt has more volume than table salt, which means you may need to use a touch more in your recipes.

- *Ground black pepper*

- *Garlic powder*

- *Paprika*

- *Chicken seasoning or rub:* My go-to chicken seasoning mix is McCormick Grill Mates Montreal Chicken. This shake-on spice mixture can be used to season meat even if you are not grilling. It can be found in most grocery stores in the spice aisle. However, any chicken rub or chicken seasoning is fine. The seasoning typically includes salt, pepper, sage, thyme, paprika, garlic powder, and onion powder.

- *Taco seasoning:* This provides immensely spicy flavor for empanadas, fajitas, and more.

- *Italian seasoning:* This is normally a combination of rosemary, thyme, oregano, basil, marjoram, and red pepper flakes.

- *Hamburger seasoning:* McCormick and Weber both offer great burger seasoning. The ingredients include garlic, onion, sugar, and Worcestershire.

- *Ground cinnamon*

- *Stevia:* Stevia is an organic, sugar-free, zero-calorie sweetener and is used as a substitute for refined sugar. Stevia can be found in most grocery stores. It is typically located in the baking aisle near the refined sugar. You will find stevia listed as an ingredient throughout this cookbook. In these instances, refined sugar is suggested as a substitute along with serving-size conversion. I made the switch from using refined sugar due to the associated health risks and have opted to use stevia because it is plant based. However, some people with common hay fever allergies, such as goldenrod, are allergic to stevia; make sure you know your body's reaction before you make your sweetener decisions.

- *Sugar:* If you choose to use sugar, consider evaporated cane juice instead of plain white table sugar. It is less refined and has a slightly lower glycemic index.

- *Honey:* Local honey is always best! There's been a bit of a honey renaissance these past few years. Do a little poking around your farmers' market for a brand that supports your local apiary.

Step-by-Step Air-Frying

1. Before using your air fryer for the first time, read the instruction manual that is provided.

2. Remove all packaging material and stickers from the appliance. Open the drawer and remove the basket, pan, and any cardboard packaging.

3. Clean the air fryer basket and pan using hot water. Return the basket and pan to the drawer. Slide the drawer back into the air fryer.

4. Place the air fryer on a level surface. Do not place the air fryer under objects that can be damaged by heat or steam. Do not place anything on top of the air fryer. Remember, your air fryer relies on air flow.

5. Plug the unit into an outlet.

6. For most models, preheating the air fryer is not required. If you wish to do so, set the timer for 5 minutes. Allow the machine to run. When the timer sounds, the set time has elapsed.

7. If you plan to use accessories with the air fryer, it is best to place them securely in the air fryer before the heat is turned on. (You do not want to stick your hands into the basket while the unit is hot.)

8. To remove food from the air fryer, lift out the air fryer basket from the drawer. Do not turn the air fryer drawer upside down.

9. Clean the appliance after every use. Wipe any oil from the bottom of the drip pan after each cooking process to minimize the risk of the appliance smoking. Never use steel wool to clean the air fryer, as this will damage the air fryer basket. Most models are dishwasher safe.

Air Fryer Troubleshooting

WHITE SMOKE

White smoke may surface from your air fryer for a variety of reasons. If you are preparing food that is high in fat, the food may produce excess oil, which lingers in the air fryer. You may need to check in during the cooking process and soak up any excess oil with a paper towel. Once the oil is cleaned up, resume cooking. White smoke will not harm the air fryer. Smoke may also surface if the air fryer is not properly cleaned in between each use. Check to ensure there isn't any oil left in the bottom of the air fryer from previous use.

BLACK SMOKE

Black smoke should not surface from your air fryer. If you notice black smoke, turn off and unplug the machine immediately, and consult with the manufacturer.

NOT CRISPING

If you notice that your food is not browning or becoming crisp, you may not have added enough oil. Try adding a little additional oil. Make sure you have not over-crowded the air fryer basket and that you have flipped food repeatedly throughout the cooking process.

A LITTLE SPRITZ WILL DO YA

When air-frying, you usually need to spritz your food with a little oil. Air fryers get very hot and blow around air. They do no ventilate smoke very well. Oils that have a higher smoke point, such as extra-virgin olive, canola, avocado, and grapeseed, are ideal. I typically use extra-virgin olive oil in a spray bottle. This makes it very easy to spritz oil directly on your food. My go-to is the Evo Oil Sprayer bottle. It has an aerosol-free trigger that sprays in a fan-shaped pattern to allow for precise application. It can be found online and from various retailers.

You will find most recipes require only about a tablespoon of oil. This significantly cuts down on the fat found in most deep-fried foods. Olive, canola (expeller-pressed only), avocado, and grapeseed oils are great sources of monounsaturated fat, aka "the good fats." Monounsaturated fat may help lower risk of heart disease by improving risk factors.

Air Fryer Cooking Charts: Fresh and Frozen Food

FAVORITE FROZEN FOOD COOKING CHART

FROZEN FOOD	QUANTITY	TIME	TEMPERATURE	NOTES
Breaded shrimp	Up to 1 pound	8 to 10 minutes	400°F	*Spray with oil and flip halfway through cooking*
Chicken nuggets	1 to 4 cups	10 to 15 minutes	400°F	*Spray with oil and shake halfway through cooking*
Fish fillets	¼ to 1 pound	14 to 15 minutes	400°F	*Spray with oil and flip halfway through cooking*
Fish sticks	¼ to 1 pound	6 to 10 minutes	400°F	*Spray with oil and shake halfway through cooking*
Hash browns	1 to 2 cups	15 to 18 minutes	370°F	*Spray with oil and shake halfway through cooking*
Onion rings	1 pound	8 to 10 minutes	400°F	*Spray with oil and flip halfway through cooking*
Tater tots	1¼ to 3 cups	10 to 12 minutes	400°F	*Spray with oil and shake halfway through cooking*
Thick fries	1¼ to 3 cups	18 to 20 minutes	400°F	*Spray with oil and shake halfway through cooking*
Thin fries	1¼ to 3 cups	14 minutes	400°F	*Spray with oil and shake halfway through cooking*

FROZEN FOOD	QUANTITY	TIME	TEMPERATURE	NOTES
Burgers	¼ to 1 pound	14 to 15 minutes	400°F	*Do not stack; flip half-way through cooking*
Burritos	2 burritos	8 to 10 minutes	400°F	*Spray with oil and flip halfway through cooking*
Egg rolls	6 to 8 egg rolls	3 to 6 minutes	390°F	*Brush or spray with oil before cooking*
Meatballs	Up to 25 meatballs	8 to 10 minutes	380°F	*Flip halfway through cooking*
Mozzarella sticks	¼ to 1 pound	8 to 10 minutes	360°F	*Spray with oil and flip halfway through cooking*
Pizza	1 pizza	5 to 10 minutes	390°F	*Place pizza on parchment paper; make sure it fits in the basket*
Pizza bagels	4 or 5 pizza bagels	8 to 10 minutes	375°F	*Spray with oil; do not stack*
Pizza rolls (bites)	10 pizza rolls	5 to 7 minutes	375°F	*Spray with oil and shake halfway through cooking*
Pot stickers	1 to 3 cups	8 to 10 minutes	400°F	*Spray with oil and flip halfway through cooking*
Samosas	6 to 8 samosas	5 to 10 minutes	400°F	*Spray with oil and shake halfway through cooking*

FRESH FOOD COOKING CHART

FRESH VEGETABLES	QUANTITY	TIME	TEMPERATURE	NOTES
Asparagus	1 pound	5 to 8 minutes	400°F	*Trim the ends before cooking*
Broccoli	2 to 4 cups	5 to 8 minutes	400°F	*Season with salt and pepper; spray with oil*
Brussels sprouts	2 cups	13 to 15 minutes	380°F	*Cut the Brussels sprouts in half lengthwise first; coat with oil and seasonings*
Carrots	1 to 2 cups	7 to 10 minutes	380°F	*Cut first*
Cauliflower florets	2 to 4 cups	9 to 10 minutes	360°F	*Coat with oil and seasonings*
Corn on the cob	4 ears	6 minutes	390°F	*Coat with oil and seasonings*
Eggplant	1 to 3 pounds	13 to 15 minutes	400°F	*Spray with oil and flip halfway through cooking*
Green beans	1 to 3 pounds	5 minutes	400°F	*Spray with oil and shake halfway through cooking*
Kale	1 bunch	10 to 12 minutes	275°F	*Trim leaves from ribs; coat with oil and sprinkle with seasonings*
Mushrooms	1 to 2 cups	5 to 8 minutes	400°F	*Trim stems first*
Onions	1 to 3 pounds	5 to 8 minutes	370°F	*Chop first*
Peppers (bell)	1 to 2 cups	6 to 8 minutes	370°F	*Cut into strips first*

FRESH VEGETABLES	QUANTITY	TIME	TEMPERATURE	NOTES
Potatoes (baked)	3 or 4 potatoes	40 minutes	400°F	*Poke holes or cut slits along the top first*
Potatoes (cubed)	1 ¼ to 3 cups	15 minutes	400°F	*Spray with oil and shake halfway through cooking*
Potatoes (fries)	1 ¼ to 3 cups	15 minutes	380°F	*Spray with oil and shake halfway through cooking*
Potatoes (wedges)	2 to 4 cups	18 to 20 minutes	380°F	*Spray with oil and shake halfway through cooking*
Squash	1 pound	12 to 13 minutes	400°F	*Brush with cooking oil and seasonings*
Sweet potatoes (baked)	2 sweet potatoes	35 to 40 minutes	390°F	*Poke holes or cut a slit through the top of each potato prior to cooking*
Sweet potatoes (cubed)	3 to 5 cups	14 to 20 minutes	380°F	*Spray with oil and shake halfway through cooking*
Sweet potatoes (fries)	1 ¼ to 3 cups	25 minutes	380°F	*Spray with oil and shake halfway through cooking*
Tomatoes (breaded)	1 to 3 pounds	10 minutes	350°F	*Cut first and apply breading*
Zucchini	1 to 3 pounds	10 to 12 minutes	370°F	*Cut first*

CHICKEN	QUANTITY	TIME	TEMPERATURE	NOTES
Chicken breasts (boneless, skinless)	Up to 4 (6-ounce) breasts	12 to 15 minutes	380°F	*Spray with oil and flip halfway through cooking*
Chicken drumettes	Up to 8 drumettes	20 minutes	400°F	*Spray with oil and shake halfway through cooking*
Chicken drumsticks	1 to 6 drumsticks	16 to 20 minutes	390°F	*Spray with oil and shake halfway through cooking*
Chicken thighs (bone-in)	Up to 4 (6-ounce) thighs	22 minutes	380°F	*Spray with oil and shake halfway through cooking*
Chicken thighs (boneless)	Up to 4 (6-ounce) thighs	18 to 20 minutes	380°F	*Spray with oil and shake halfway through cooking*
Chicken tenders	Up to 8 tenders	8 to 10 minutes	375°F	*Spray with oil and shake halfway through cooking*
Chicken wings	Up to 8 wings	15 to 20 minutes	400°F	*Spray with oil and shake halfway through cooking*
Whole chicken	2 pounds	75 minutes	360°F	*Coat with oil and seasonings*

BEEF	QUANTITY	TIME	TEMPERATURE	NOTES
Burgers	¼ to 1 pound	8 to 10 minutes	400°F	*Do not stack; flip halfway through cooking*
Filet mignon	Up to 4 (6-ounce) steaks	8 to 10 minutes	360°F	*Time will vary depending on desired doneness; use a meat thermometer and cook to 125°F for rare, 135°F for medium-rare, 145°F for medium, 155°F for medium-well, and 160° F for well-done*
Flank steak	¼ to 1 pound	8 to 10 minutes	360°F	*Time will vary depending on desired doneness; use a meat thermometer and cook to 125°F for rare, 135°F for medium-rare, 145°F for medium, 155°F for medium-well, and 160°F for well-done*
Meatballs	Up to 25 meatballs	7 to 10 minutes	380°F	*Flip halfway through cooking*
Ribeye	Up to 4 (6-ounce) steaks	10 to 15 minutes	380°F	*Time will vary depending on desired doneness; use a meat thermometer and cook to 125°F for rare, 135°F for medium-rare, 145°F for medium, 155°F for medium-well, and 160°F for well-done*
Sirloin steak	Up to 4 (6-ounce) steaks	12 to 14 minutes	400°F	*Time will vary depending on desired doneness; use a meat thermometer and cook to 125°F for rare, 135°F for medium-rare, 145°F for medium, 155°F for medium-well, and 160°F for well-done*

PORK AND LAMB	QUANTITY	TIME	TEMPERATURE	NOTES
Bacon	6 slices	7 to 10 minutes	400°F	*Flip halfway through cooking*
Lamb chops	¼ to 1 pound	10 to 12 minutes	400°F	*Do not stack; flip halfway through cooking*
Pork chops (bone-in or boneless)	¼ to 1 pound	12 to 15 minutes	380°F	*Spray with oil and flip halfway through to evenly distribute*
Pork loin	¼ to 1 pound	50 to 60 minutes	360°F	*Sprinkle with seasonings and flip halfway through cooking*
Pork tenderloin	¼ to 1 pound	12 to 15 minutes	390°F	*Drizzle with olive oil and cook whole*
Rack of lamb	¼ to 1 pound	22 to 25 minutes	380°F	*Do not stack; flip halfway through cooking*
Sausage (links)	¼ to 1 pound	13 to 15 minutes	380°F	*Pierce holes in sausages first*
Sausage (patties)	Up to 6 patties	13 to 15 minutes	380°F	*Flip halfway through cooking*

FISH AND SEAFOOD	QUANTITY	TIME	TEMPERATURE	NOTES
Crab cakes	4 crab cakes	8 to 10 minutes	375°F	*Toss with all-purpose flour and coat with oil*
Fish fillets	¼ to 1 pound	10 to 12 minutes	320°F	*Brush with oil and sprinkle with seasonings*
Scallops	¼ to 1 pound	5 to 7 minutes	320°F	*Brush with oil and sprinkle with seasonings*
Shrimp	¼ to 1 pound	7 to 8 minutes	400°F	*Peel and devein; brush with oil and sprinkle with seasonings*

FRESH FRUIT	QUANTITY	TIME	TEMPERATURE	NOTES
Apples	2 to 4 cups	4 to 7 minutes	350°F	*Cut first*
Bananas	2 to 4 cups	4 to 7 minutes	350°F	*Cut first*
Peaches	2 to 4 cups	5 to 6 minutes	350°F	*Cut first*

Ten Tips for Perfect Air-Frying Every Time

1. Invest in an oil sprayer bottle. As mentioned previously, most of the recipes in this cookbook will require a small amount of oil. Using an oil sprayer makes the process very convenient. I prefer the Evo bottle.

2. Preheat your air fryer if it is recommended for your model. This step will vary based on the air fryer brand that you use. I have the Power AirFryer. The included manual states that preheating is not necessary. If your brand requires preheating, turn the air fryer on and let it run for 4 to 5 minutes before use.

3. Do not overcrowd the air fryer basket. While cooking, you should be conscious of your air fryer size and be careful not to place too much food in the machine at once. Crowding will prevent foods from properly browning and becoming crisp. Cooking in batches is sometimes the ideal plan.

4. Open the air fryer while the food is cooking to monitor doneness. I open my air fryer several times during the cooking process to ensure the food does not over-cook. Closely monitoring your food allows you to have more control over the end results. When you close the air fryer, it will resume cooking and the time will pick up where it left off.

5. Use proper breading. Many recipes in this cookbook include the ingredients and steps necessary for breading. You will want to first coat foods in flour, then egg (or egg whites), and then bread crumbs. When breading, spray cooking oil from a distance. If you spray oil directly onto your food, the bread crumbs may go flying.

6. Frozen foods require more attention than most recipes (refer to the Favorite Frozen Food Cooking Chart on page 14). I also recommend that you open the air fryer throughout the cooking process to monitor doneness.

7. Shake the air fryer basket so that foods are fully cooked. Recipes for items like chicken wings and fries will require shaking. It is fine to stack these items in the air fryer (do no overcrowd), but you will have to open the air fryer during the cooking process and shake the basket so that the food moves around and is evenly cooked.

8. Flip foods over midway through the cooking process. Some recipes in this cookbook will require you to flip foods over to ensure they brown evenly. You should flip items like fish and pastries as opposed to shaking the basket. This ensures your food stays intact.

9. Spray foods with additional oil if you would like your food to brown or crisp more. Sometimes, if you spray the food with cooking oil after you have placed it in the air fryer, the oil is not evenly distributed. If you notice your food is not crisping, try a little more oil.

10. Reheat food in the air fryer. If you are looking for crunchy leftovers with these recipes, use your air fryer instead of the microwave. A few minutes is all you need for it to crisp back up.

About the Recipes

A few accessories are used in the preparation of some recipes in this cookbook:

▷ Barrel pan is used for recipes like fried rice.

▷ Grill pan can be used for hamburgers and steak.

▷ Layer rack is used to make kabobs.

If your air fryer doesn't come with these accessories, they can be easily found online or at your local kitchen supply store.

The recipes featured in this cookbook are simple and easy to prepare. Sixty-two recipes can be prepared in 30 minutes or less. Most recipes include everyday ingredients that can be found in your kitchen and pantry, making it a snap to whip up weeknight dinners.

All recipes include nutrition information:

▷ Serving size

▷ Calories

▷ Total fat

▷ Saturated fat

▷ Cholesterol

▷ Sodium

▷ Carbohydrates

▷ Fiber

▷ Protein

The following labels are applied to each recipe to help categorize and give you a quick snapshot of the recipe's attributes:

- Fast (30 minutes or less, start to finish)
- Family Favorite (recipes that can feed a family of 4 and that kids and picky eaters will love)
- Vegetarian
- Gluten-Free
- Brandi's Favorite (personal family favorites and recipes I prepare often)

At the top of each recipe you'll also see how it will be prepared in the air fryer: Fry, Bake, Grill, or Roast.

Some recipes will include an "Aren't You Glad You Didn't Deep-Fry?" sidebar where I will call attention to the difference between the air-fried, healthier version of the recipe in comparison to its deep-fried counterpart.

Most recipes will also include helpful cooking, ingredient, substitution, or air fryer cooking tips so you can spend less time fussing over your meal and more time enjoying it!

Homemade Cherry Breakfast Tarts, page 32

CHAPTER 3

Breakfast

Sausage and Egg Breakfast Burrito

FAMILY FAVORITE

FRY: 400°F • PREP TIME: 5 MINUTES • COOK TIME: 30 MINUTES • SERVES 6

Nobody likes a soggy burrito! These protein-packed breakfast burritos stay crispy thanks to the air fryer. I prep my burritos in advance and air-fry them in the morning for a hearty grab-and-go breakfast. Any sausage will do; I prefer chicken since it's a healthier option.

6 eggs

Salt

Pepper

Cooking oil

½ cup chopped red bell pepper

½ cup chopped green bell pepper

8 ounces ground chicken sausage

½ cup salsa

6 medium (8-inch) flour tortillas

½ cup shredded Cheddar cheese

1. In a medium bowl, whisk the eggs. Add salt and pepper to taste.

2. Place a skillet on medium-high heat. Spray with cooking oil. Add the eggs. Scramble for 2 to 3 minutes, until the eggs are fluffy. Remove the eggs from the skillet and set aside.

3. If needed, spray the skillet with more oil. Add the chopped red and green bell peppers. Cook for 2 to 3 minutes, until the peppers are soft.

4. Add the ground sausage to the skillet. Break the sausage into smaller pieces using a spatula or spoon. Cook for 3 to 4 minutes, until the sausage is brown.

5. Add the salsa and scrambled eggs. Stir to combine. Remove the skillet from heat.

6. Spoon the mixture evenly onto the tortillas.

7. To form the burritos, fold the sides of each tortilla in toward the middle and then roll up from the bottom. You can secure each burrito with a toothpick. Or you can moisten the outside edge of the tortilla with a small amount of water. I prefer to use a cooking brush, but you can also dab with your fingers.

8. Spray the burritos with cooking oil and place them in the air fryer. Do not stack. Cook the burritos in batches if they do not all fit in the basket. Cook for 8 minutes.

9. Open the air fryer and flip the burritos. Cook for an additional 2 minutes or until crisp.

10. If necessary, repeat steps 8 and 9 for the remaining burritos.
11. Sprinkle the Cheddar cheese over the burritos. Cool before serving.

Ingredient tip: I recommend using block cheese from the dairy section of your grocery store. Bagged, preshredded cheese doesn't melt as well as cheese you shred yourself with a grater.

Per serving: Calories: 236; Total fat: 13g; Saturated fat: 5g; Cholesterol: 174mg; Sodium: 439mg; Carbohydrates: 16g; Fiber: 2g; Protein: 15g

French Toast Sticks

FAST, FAMILY FAVORITE, VEGETARIAN

FRY: 375°F • PREP TIME: 5 MINUTES • COOK TIME: 15 MINUTES
MAKES 12 STICKS (1 STICK = 1 SERVING)

Classic French toast gets a mini makeover with this breakfast treat you can eat with your fingers. If you don't have Texas toast, use any bread you have on hand. The end result is still a mouthwatering combination of crunchy and soft, buttery and sweet.

4 slices Texas toast
(or any thick bread, such
as challah)

1 tablespoon butter

1 egg

1 teaspoon stevia

1 teaspoon ground
cinnamon

¼ cup milk

1 teaspoon vanilla extract

Cooking oil

1. Cut each slice of bread into 3 pieces (for 12 sticks total).

2. Place the butter in a small, microwave-safe bowl. Microwave for 15 seconds, or until the butter has melted.

3. Remove the bowl from the microwave. Add the egg, stevia, cinnamon, milk, and vanilla extract. Whisk until fully combined.

4. Spray the air fryer basket with cooking oil.

5. Dredge each of the bread sticks in the egg mixture.

6. Place the French toast sticks in the air fryer. It is okay to stack them. Spray the French toast sticks with cooking oil. Cook for 8 minutes.

7. Open the air fryer and flip each of the French toast sticks. Cook for an additional 4 minutes, or until the French toast sticks are crisp.

8. Cool before serving.

Substitution tip: No stevia? No problem. Replace with 2 tablespoons sugar.

Per serving: Calories: 52; Total fat: 2g; Saturated fat: 1g; Cholesterol: 17mg; Sodium: 81mg; Carbohydrates: 7g; Fiber: 0g; Protein: 2g

Home-Fried Potatoes

FAMILY FAVORITE, VEGETARIAN, GLUTEN-FREE

FRY: 370°F • PREP TIME: 5 MINUTES, PLUS 30 MINUTES TO
SOAK • COOK TIME: 25 MINUTES • SERVES 4

BRANDI'S
FAVORITE
★

Home fries are my favorite breakfast or brunch side dish. Cooking them in the air fryer means less effort for the same delicious result. Here you get the same bold flavors you find in your local diner home fries, but without all of the fat and grease!

3 large russet potatoes

1 tablespoon canola oil

1 tablespoon extra-virgin olive oil

1 teaspoon paprika

Salt

Pepper

1 cup chopped onion

1 cup chopped red bell pepper

1 cup chopped green bell pepper

1. Cut the potatoes into ½-inch cubes. Place the potatoes in a large bowl of cold water and allow them to soak for at least 30 minutes, preferably an hour.

2. Drain the potatoes and dry thoroughly with paper towels. Return them to the empty bowl.

3. Add the canola and olive oils, paprika, and salt and pepper to taste. Toss to fully coat the potatoes.

4. Transfer the potatoes to the air fryer. Cook for 20 minutes, shaking the air fryer basket every 5 minutes (a total of 4 times).

5. Add the onion and red and green bell peppers to the air fryer basket. Cook for an additional 3 to 4 minutes, or until the potatoes are cooked through and the peppers are soft.

6. Cool before serving.

Cooking tip: Check on the potatoes frequently; use a fork to test if the potatoes are soft and have finished cooking.

Per serving: Calories: 279; Total fat: 8g; Saturated fat: 1g; Cholesterol: 0mg; Sodium: 58mg; Carbohydrates: 50g; Fiber: 8g; Protein: 6g

Homemade Cherry Breakfast Tarts

FAMILY FAVORITE, VEGETARIAN

BAKE: 375°F • PREP TIME: 15 MINUTES • COOK TIME: 20 MINUTES • SERVES 6

These kid-friendly breakfast tarts also make a wonderful breakfast treat for adults! The crispy crust paired with the warm, sweet-tart filling feels like the ultimate indulgence. For a less sweet version, you can omit the frosting. Either way, once you make your own homemade breakfast tarts, you will never look to store-bought again.

For the tarts

2 refrigerated piecrusts

⅓ cup cherry preserves

1 teaspoon cornstarch

Cooking oil

For the frosting

½ cup vanilla yogurt

1 ounce cream cheese

1 teaspoon stevia

Rainbow sprinkles

To make the tarts

1. Place the piecrusts on a flat surface. Using a knife or pizza cutter, cut each piecrust into 3 rectangles, for 6 total. (I discard the unused dough left from slicing the edges.)

2. In a small bowl, combine the preserves and cornstarch. Mix well.

3. Scoop 1 tablespoon of the preserves mixture onto the top half of each piece of piecrust.

4. Fold the bottom of each piece up to close the tart. Using the back of a fork, press along the edges of each tart to seal.

5. Spray the breakfast tarts with cooking oil and place them in the air fryer. I do not recommend stacking the breakfast tarts. They will stick together if stacked. You may need to prepare them in two batches. Cook for 10 minutes.

6. Allow the breakfast tarts to cool fully before removing from the air fryer.

7. If necessary, repeat steps 5 and 6 for the remaining breakfast tarts.

To make the frosting

1. In a small bowl, combine the yogurt, cream cheese, and stevia. Mix well.

2. Spread the breakfast tarts with frosting and top with sprinkles, and serve.

Substitution tip: Greek vanilla yogurt can be used in this recipe in place of the vanilla yogurt and is a great option for 8 additional grams of protein. If you prefer sugar, swap 2 teaspoons sugar for the stevia.

Cooking tip: Check in on the breakfast tarts after 7 or 8 minutes to ensure they are not too crisp. For softer breakfast tarts, allow them to cook until they turn light brown. For crispier breakfast tarts, cook until they are golden brown.

Per serving: Calories: 119; Total fat: 4g; Saturated fat: 2g; Cholesterol: 8mg; Sodium: 81mg; Carbohydrates: 19g; Fiber: 0g; Protein: 2g

Sausage and Cream Cheese Biscuits

FAST, FAMILY FAVORITE

FRY: 370°F • PREP TIME: 5 MINUTES • COOK TIME: 15 MINUTES • SERVES 5

This recipe reminds me of biscuits and gravy, but a modern, on-the-go version! Breakfast sandwiches make a great option for when you don't have time to sit down for a meal. By cooking them in the air fryer, you can focus on the richness of these flavors without worrying about dripping grease while you eat. Any sausage will work here.

12 ounces chicken breakfast sausage

1 (6-ounce) can biscuits

⅛ cup cream cheese

1. Form the sausage into 5 small patties.
2. Place the sausage patties in the air fryer. Cook for 5 minutes.
3. Open the air fryer. Flip the patties. Cook for an additional 5 minutes.
4. Remove the cooked sausages from the air fryer.
5. Separate the biscuit dough into 5 biscuits.
6. Place the biscuits in the air fryer. Cook for 3 minutes.
7. Open the air fryer. Flip the biscuits. Cook for an additional 2 minutes.
8. Remove the cooked biscuits from the air fryer.
9. Split each biscuit in half. Spread 1 teaspoon of cream cheese onto the bottom of each biscuit. Top with a sausage patty and the other half of the biscuit, and serve.

Substitution tip: Using reduced-fat cream cheese will save some calories in this recipe.

Cooking tip: Check the inside of the sausage to ensure it is no longer pink and has fully cooked through.

Per serving: Calories: 249; Total fat: 13g; Saturated fat: 7g; Cholesterol: 6mg; Sodium: 556mg; Carbohydrates: 20g; Fiber: 0g; Protein: 9g

Fried Chicken and Waffles

FAMILY FAVORITE

FRY: 400°F (CHICKEN) / 370°F (WAFFLES)
PREP TIME: 10 MINUTES • COOK TIME: 30 MINUTES • SERVES 4

I first heard about chicken and waffles while watching '90s sitcoms. Roscoe's Chicken and Waffles was mentioned as a well-known establishment on the West Coast that served this dish up as its specialty. As a child, I was intrigued. Savory dinner dishes never appeared at our breakfast table. As a brunch connoisseur, I fully understand this pairing now. The sweet-and-savory combination is unmatched—don't knock it until you try it!

8 whole chicken wings

1 teaspoon garlic powder

Chicken seasoning or rub

Pepper

½ cup all-purpose flour

Cooking oil

8 frozen waffles

Maple syrup (optional)

AREN'T YOU GLAD YOU DIDN'T DEEP-FRY?

A fried chicken breast and large waffle commonly served at restaurants amount to about 941 calories.

---

1. In a medium bowl, season the chicken with the garlic powder and chicken seasoning and pepper to taste.

2. Transfer the chicken to a sealable plastic bag and add the flour. Shake to thoroughly coat the chicken.

3. Spray the air fryer basket with cooking oil.

4. Using tongs, transfer the chicken from the bag to the air fryer. It is okay to stack the chicken wings on top of each other. Spray them with cooking oil. Cook for 5 minutes.

5. Open the air fryer and shake the basket. Continue to cook the chicken. Repeat shaking every 5 minutes until 20 minutes has passed and the chicken is fully cooked.

6. Remove the cooked chicken from the air fryer and set aside.

7. Rinse the basket and base out with warm water. Return them to the air fryer.

8. Reduce the temperature of the air fryer to 370°F.

9. Place the frozen waffles in the air fryer. Do not stack. Depending on the size of your air fryer, you may need to cook the waffles in batches. Spray the waffles with cooking oil. Cook for 6 minutes.

10. If necessary, remove the cooked waffles from the air fryer, then repeat step 9 for the remaining waffles.

11. Serve the waffles with the chicken and a touch of maple syrup if desired.

Per serving: Calories: 461; Total fat: 22g; Saturated fat: 5g; Cholesterol: 95mg; Sodium: 567mg; Carbohydrates: 45g; Fiber: 2g; Protein: 28g

Cheesy Tater Tot Breakfast Bake

FAST, FAMILY FAVORITE

BAKE: 400°F • PREP TIME: 5 MINUTES • COOK TIME: 20 MINUTES • SERVES 4

If you have ever wanted to sneak protein into a dish while feeding children, this kid-approved tater tot bake should do the trick! Perfect for a lazy weekend brunch, kids and adults alike will devour this dish. You will need a barrel pan accessory for this recipe, and any sausage will work fine.

4 eggs

1 cup milk

1 teaspoon onion powder

Salt

Pepper

Cooking oil

12 ounces ground chicken sausage

1 pound frozen tater tots

¾ cup shredded Cheddar cheese

1. In a medium bowl, whisk the eggs. Add the milk, onion powder, and salt and pepper to taste. Stir to combine.

2. Spray a skillet with cooking oil and set over medium-high heat. Add the ground sausage. Using a spatula or spoon, break the sausage into smaller pieces. Cook for 3 to 4 minutes, until the sausage is brown. Remove from heat and set aside.

3. Spray a barrel pan with cooking oil. Make sure to cover the bottom and sides of the pan.

4. Place the tater tots in the barrel pan. Cook for 6 minutes.

5. Open the air fryer and shake the pan, then add the egg mixture and cooked sausage. Cook for an additional 6 minutes.

6. Open the air fryer and sprinkle the cheese over the tater tot bake. Cook for an additional 2 to 3 minutes.

7. Cool before serving.

Substitution tip: Egg whites can be substituted for the whole eggs to reduce calories and fat. If using store-bought liquid egg whites, ½ cup is comparable to 4 egg whites.

Cooking tip: Eight minutes should create light and fluffy eggs. If you prefer firmer eggs, cook for 10 minutes, or until your eggs are fully set.

Per serving: Calories: 518; Total fat: 30g; Saturated fat: 11g; Cholesterol: 263mg; Sodium: 757mg; Carbohydrates: 31g; Fiber: 3g; Protein: 30g

Breakfast Scramble Casserole

FAST, FAMILY FAVORITE, GLUTEN-FREE

BAKE: 400°F • PREP TIME: 20 MINUTES • COOK TIME: 10 MINUTES • SERVES 4

Packed with crunchy bacon, delicious chopped vegetables, and melted cheese, this protein-rich casserole makes for a great low-carb breakfast. I love casseroles because you throw the ingredients in a pan and simply wait for the food to bake. The air fryer saves 30 minutes of time in comparison to oven-baked casseroles. You will need a barrel pan accessory for this recipe.

6 slices bacon

6 eggs

Salt

Pepper

Cooking oil

½ cup chopped red bell pepper

½ cup chopped green bell pepper

½ cup chopped onion

¾ cup shredded Cheddar cheese

1. In a skillet over medium-high heat, cook the bacon, 5 to 7 minutes, flipping to evenly crisp. Drain on paper towels, crumble, and set aside.

2. In a medium bowl, whisk the eggs. Add salt and pepper to taste.

3. Spray a barrel pan with cooking oil. Make sure to cover the bottom and sides of the pan.

4. Add the beaten eggs, crumbled bacon, red bell pepper, green bell pepper, and onion to the pan. Place the pan in the air fryer. Cook for 6 minutes.

5. Open the air fryer and sprinkle the cheese over the casserole. Cook for an additional 2 minutes.

6. Cool before serving.

Substitution tip: Egg whites can be substituted for whole eggs for fewer calories and less fat. If using store-bought liquid egg whites, 1 cup is comparable to 6 egg whites.

Cooking tip: Eight minutes should create light and fluffy eggs. If you believe your eggs need additional time to cook, cook for 10 minutes, or until the eggs are fully set.

Per serving: Calories: 348; Total fat: 26g; Saturated fat: 11g; Cholesterol: 299mg; Sodium: 922mg; Carbohydrates: 4g; Fiber: 1g; Protein: 25g

Breakfast Grilled Ham and Cheese

FAST, FAMILY FAVORITE

BAKE: 370°F • PREP TIME: 5 MINUTES • COOK TIME: 10 MINUTES • SERVES 2

This savory grilled cheese isn't for lunch; it was made for breakfast! Growing up, grilled cheese and tomato soup were a staple in our home. This version includes smoked country ham, thick-sliced tomato, and of course, gooey melted cheese. You use a lot less butter cooking this in an air fryer—it cuts out half of the calories and fat.

1 teaspoon butter

4 slices bread

4 slices smoked
   country ham

4 slices Cheddar cheese

4 thick slices tomato

1. Spread ½ teaspoon of butter onto one side of 2 slices of bread. Each sandwich will have 1 slice of bread with butter and 1 slice without.

2. Assemble each sandwich by layering 2 slices of ham, 2 slices of cheese, and 2 slices of tomato on the unbuttered pieces of bread. Top with the other bread slices, buttered side up.

3. Place the sandwiches in the air fryer buttered-side down. Cook for 4 minutes.

4. Open the air fryer. Flip the grilled cheese sandwiches. Cook for an additional 4 minutes.

5. Cool before serving. Cut each sandwich in half and enjoy.

Substitution tip: Any type of ham works well for this recipe, so use what you have on hand. White Cheddar cheese tastes delicious in this sandwich.

Air fryer cooking tip: If the top slice of bread moves around inside the air fryer while cooking, secure it with a toothpick.

Per serving: Calories: 525; Total fat: 25g; Saturated fat: 14g; Cholesterol: 88mg; Sodium: 1618mg; Carbohydrates: 34g; Fiber: 5g; Protein: 41g

Classic Hash Browns

FAMILY FAVORITE, VEGETARIAN, GLUTEN-FREE

FRY: 370°F • PREP TIME: 15 MINUTES • COOK TIME: 20 MINUTES • SERVES 4

Making homemade hash browns is a cinch. All you need is a vegetable peeler and a cheese grater. These potatoes are crispy on the outside and fluffy on the inside.

4 russet potatoes

1 teaspoon paprika

Salt

Pepper

Cooking oil

AREN'T YOU GLAD YOU DIDN'T DEEP-FRY?

If you order breakfast hash browns in a diner, you are looking at about 27 grams of fat per serving. The air fryer cuts that!

1. Peel the potatoes using a vegetable peeler. Using a cheese grater, shred the potatoes. If your grater has different-size holes, use the area of the tool with the largest holes.

2. Place the shredded potatoes in a large bowl of cold water. Let sit for 5 minutes. Cold water helps remove excess starch from the potatoes. Stir to help dissolve the starch.

3. Drain the potatoes and dry with paper towels or napkins. Make sure the potatoes are completely dry.

4. Season the potatoes with the paprika and salt and pepper to taste.

5. Spray the potatoes with cooking oil and transfer them to the air fryer. Cook for 20 minutes, shaking the basket every 5 minutes (a total of 4 times).

6. Cool before serving.

Per serving: Calories: 150; Total fat: 0g; Saturated fat: 0g; Cholesterol: 0mg; Sodium: 52mg; Carbohydrates: 34g; Fiber: 5g; Protein: 4g

Canadian Bacon and Cheese English Muffins

FAST, FAMILY FAVORITE

BAKE: 370°F • PREP TIME: 5 MINUTES • COOK TIME: 10 MINUTES • SERVES 4

Are you craving bacon but are pressed for time? Here is a quick sandwich that is rich in flavor. Simply toasting your English muffin will not cut it if you own an air fryer! This sandwich delivers a powerful crunch not achieved with a toaster.

4 English muffins

8 slices Canadian bacon

4 slices cheese

Cooking oil

1. Split each English muffin. Assemble the breakfast sandwiches by layering 2 slices of Canadian bacon and 1 slice of cheese onto each English muffin bottom. Top with the other half of the English muffin.

2. Place the sandwiches in the air fryer. Spray the top of each with cooking oil. Cook for 4 minutes.

3. Open the air fryer and flip the sandwiches. Cook for an additional 4 minutes.

4. Cool before serving.

Ingredient tip: Whole-wheat English muffins provide a healthy alternative.

Per serving: Calories: 333; Total fat: 14g; Saturated fat: 8g; Cholesterol: 58mg; Sodium: 1219mg; Carbohydrates: 27g; Fiber: 2g; Protein: 24g

Classic French Fries, page 44

CHAPTER 4

Snacks and Appetizers

Classic French Fries

FAMILY FAVORITE, VEGETARIAN, GLUTEN-FREE

FRY: 380°F • PREP TIME: 5 MINUTES, PLUS 30 MINUTES
TO SOAK • COOK TIME: 30 MINUTES • SERVES 6

Few things compare to the mouthwatering goodness of hot and fresh French fries. These classic fries are ideal for weeknight dinners when you want to avoid fast food. So ditch the drive-through and make these at home for the family—with the air fryer, it's easier than you think.

3 large russet potatoes

1 tablespoon canola oil

1 tablespoon extra-virgin olive oil

Salt

Pepper

1. Peel the potatoes and cut lengthwise to create French fries.

2. Place the potatoes in a large bowl of cold water. Allow the potatoes to soak in the water for at least 30 minutes, preferably an hour. (See Prep tip.)

3. Spread the fries onto a baking sheet (optional: lined with parchment paper) and coat them with the canola oil, olive oil, and salt and pepper to taste.

4. Transfer half of the fries to the air fryer basket. Cook for 10 minutes.

5. Open the air fryer and shake the basket so that the fries that were at the bottom come up to the top. Cook for an additional 5 minutes.

6. When the first half finishes, remove the cooked fries, then repeat steps 4 and 5 for the remaining fries.

7. Cool before serving.

Prep tip: Soaking the potatoes in water will remove the excess starch from the potatoes. This results in crispy, crunchy fries. If you do not soak the potatoes first, they will likely turn out soft. You can prep and soak the potatoes in advance of cooking—for weeknight dinners, I do this while I prepare the main course.

Cooking tip: Use your judgment and overall preference to determine how long the fries should cook. If the fries need to be crisper, allow them to cook for additional time. Really crisp fries may need to cook up to 20 minutes. Some of this may also depend on how thick you cut your potatoes.

Per serving: Calories: 168; Total fat: 5g; Saturated fat: 1g; Cholesterol: 0mg; Sodium: 38mg; Carbohydrates: 29g; Fiber: 4g; Protein: 3g

Olive Oil Sweet Potato Chips

FAMILY FAVORITE, VEGETARIAN, GLUTEN-FREE

FRY: 400°F • PREP TIME: 10 MINUTES, PLUS 30 MINUTES
TO SOAK • COOK TIME: 20 MINUTES • SERVES 5

Chips are one of my guilty pleasures, but store-bought potato chips are bloated with calories and fat. These lighter, air-fried sweet potato chips are prepared using only five ingredients, and they have a slightly sweet and savory kick. If you prefer savory flavors, omit the cinnamon.

3 sweet potatoes

2 teaspoons extra-virgin olive oil

1 teaspoon cinnamon (optional)

Salt

Pepper

1. Peel the sweet potatoes using a vegetable peeler. Cut the potatoes crosswise into thin slices. You can also use a mandoline to slice the potatoes into chips.

2. Place the sweet potatoes in a large bowl of cold water for 30 minutes. This helps remove the starch from the sweet potatoes, which promotes crisping.

3. Drain the sweet potatoes. Dry the slices thoroughly with paper towels or napkins.

4. Place the sweet potatoes in another large bowl. Drizzle with the olive oil and sprinkle with the cinnamon, if using, and salt and pepper to taste. Toss to fully coat.

5. Place the sweet potato slices in the air fryer. It is okay to stack them, but do not overcrowd. You may need to cook the chips in two batches. Cook the potatoes for 10 minutes.

6. Open the air fryer and shake the basket. Cook the chips for an additional 10 minutes.

7. Cool before serving.

Cooking tip: Before removing all of the chips from the air fryer, test one to ensure it is crunchy and has finished cooking.

Per serving: Calories: 94; Total fat: 2g; Saturated fat: 0g; Cholesterol: 0mg; Sodium: 58mg; Carbohydrates: 20g; Fiber: 2g; Protein: 1g

Parmesan Breaded Zucchini Chips

FAMILY FAVORITE, VEGETARIAN

FRY: 350°F • PREP TIME: 15 MINUTES • COOK TIME: 20 MINUTES • SERVES 5

If you often need to sneak in green veggies the way I do, you'll love this snack. These chips are made with low-carb, nutrient-packed zucchini, which are fried with an irresistible Parmesan cheese breading. You won't be able to have just one, especially when paired with this easy lemon aioli.

For the zucchini chips

2 medium zucchini

2 eggs

⅓ cup bread crumbs

⅓ cup grated
   Parmesan cheese

Salt

Pepper

Cooking oil

For the lemon aioli

½ cup mayonnaise

½ tablespoon olive oil

Juice of ½ lemon

1 teaspoon minced garlic

Salt

Pepper

To make the zucchini chips

1. Slice the zucchini into thin chips (about ⅛ inch thick) using a knife or mandoline.

2. In a small bowl, beat the eggs. In another small bowl, combine the bread crumbs, Parmesan cheese, and salt and pepper to taste.

3. Spray the air fryer basket with cooking oil.

4. Dip the zucchini slices one at a time in the eggs and then the bread crumb mixture. You can also sprinkle the bread crumbs onto the zucchini slices with a spoon.

5. Place the zucchini chips in the air fryer basket, but do not stack. Cook in batches. Spray the chips with cooking oil from a distance (otherwise, the breading may fly off). Cook for 10 minutes.

6. Remove the cooked zucchini chips from the air fryer, then repeat step 5 with the remaining zucchini.

To make the lemon aioli

1. While the zucchini is cooking, combine the mayonnaise, olive oil, lemon juice, and garlic in a small bowl, adding salt and pepper to taste. Mix well until fully combined.

2. Cool the zucchini and serve alongside the aioli.

Cooking tip: Check in on the zucchini chips throughout the cooking process to monitor doneness and adjust cook time as necessary. The zucchini will turn deep golden brown when crisp.

Per serving (includes 2 tablespoons of aioli): Calories: 192; Total fat: 13g; Saturated fat: 3g; Cholesterol: 97mg; Sodium: 254mg; Carbohydrates: 12g; Fiber: 4g; Protein: 6g

Low-Carb Cheese-Stuffed Jalapeño Poppers

FAST, VEGETARIAN

BAKE: 370°F • PREP TIME: 10 MINUTES • COOK TIME: 5 MINUTES • SERVES 5

My friends often cringe when they see how much Sriracha I typically drizzle on my food—I just love heat! These jalapeño poppers aren't *too* spicy, but if you want to kick them up a notch, I've provided a variation. In this recipe, the peppers are hollowed out and stuffed with your favorite cheeses, then topped with bread crumbs to create a crispy crust. Can you believe this recipe is low-carb?

10 jalapeño peppers

6 ounces cream cheese

¼ cup shredded
   Cheddar cheese

2 tablespoons panko
   bread crumbs

Cooking oil

1. I recommend you wear gloves while handling jalapeños. Halve the jalapeños lengthwise. Remove the seeds and the white membrane. (Save these if you prefer spicy poppers; see Variation tip.)

2. Place the cream cheese in a small, microwave-safe bowl. Microwave for 15 seconds to soften.

3. Remove the bowl from the microwave. Add the Cheddar cheese. Mix well.

4. Stuff each of the jalapeño halves with the cheese mixture, then sprinkle the panko bread crumbs on top of each popper.

5. Place the poppers in the air fryer. Spray them with cooking oil. Cook for 5 minutes.

6. Cool before serving.

Substitution tip: Want to save some calories? Opt for reduced-fat cream cheese.

Variation tip: If you prefer five-alarm poppers, reserve the seeds and membrane when cutting the jalapeños in step 1, and add them to the cheese mixture in step 3.

Per serving: Calories: 156; Total fat: 14g; Saturated fat: 9g; Cholesterol: 43mg; Sodium: 874mg; Carbohydrates: 3g; Fiber: 1g; Protein: 4g

Vidalia Onion Blossom

FAMILY FAVORITE, VEGETARIAN

FRY: 400°F • PREP TIME: 10 MINUTES, PLUS 45 MINUTES
TO CHILL • COOK TIME: 25 MINUTES • SERVES 4

I had my first deep-fried onion blossom in high school at a Friday night football game—it was a staple at the concessions stand. You may be familiar with the Bloomin' Onion from the Outback Steakhouse menu. Now you can make your very own piping-hot restaurant-quality onion blossom without all the extra oil. This recipe is traditionally served with horseradish sauce or ranch dressing, but get creative with your dipping sauce of choice.

1 large Vidalia onion

1½ cups all-purpose flour

1 teaspoon garlic powder

1 teaspoon paprika

Salt

Pepper

2 eggs

1 cup milk

Cooking oil

1. Cut off the pointy stem end of the onion. Leave the root end intact. Peel the onion and place it cut-side down. The root end of the onion should be facing up.

2. Starting about ½ inch from the root end, cut downward to make 4 evenly spaced cuts. In each section, make 3 additional cuts. There should be 16 cuts in the onion.

3. Turn the onion over and fluff out the "petals."

4. Place the flour in a large bowl and season it with the garlic powder, paprika, and salt and pepper to taste.

5. In another large bowl, whisk the eggs. Add the milk and stir. This will form a batter.

6. Place the onion in the bowl with the flour mixture. Use a large spoon to cover the onion petals in flour.

7. Transfer the onion to the batter. Use a spoon or basting brush to cover the onion completely.

8. Return the onion to the flour mixture. Cover completely.

9. Wrap the battered onion in foil and place in the freezer for 45 minutes.

10. Spray the air fryer basket with cooking oil. Unwrap the foil covering and place the onion in the air fryer basket. Cook for 10 minutes.

11. Open the air fryer. Spray the onion with cooking oil. If areas of the onion are still white from the flour, focus the spray on these areas.

12. Cook for an additional 10 to 15 minutes, or until crisp.

Prep tip: After cutting the onion, fluff out the petals as wide as possible. This will enable you to apply breading to the inside of the onion. Be sure to fluff the petals again after freezing the onion. You want the onion to be as open as possible so that the inside cooks in the air fryer.

Cooking tip: Check the onion throughout the cooking process to monitor doneness. Cook time will vary depending on the size of the onion used. Check to see if all areas of the onion are golden brown and crisp.

Per serving: Calories: 253; Total fat: 4g; Saturated fat: 2g; Cholesterol: 87mg; Sodium: 101mg; Carbohydrates: 43g; Fiber: 2g; Protein: 10g

Crispy Fried Pickle Chips

FAST, VEGETARIAN

FRY: 400°F • PREP TIME: 10 MINUTES • COOK TIME: 10 MINUTES • SERVES 4

This simple recipe requires only five ingredients. Pickles are salty on their own, so there's no need to add salt to the breading. However, if you crave additional spice, feel free to add your go-to seasonings to the flour.

1 pound whole dill pickles

2 eggs

⅓ cup all-purpose flour

⅓ cup bread crumbs

Cooking oil

1. Cut the pickles crosswise into ½-inch-thick slices. Dry the slices completely using a paper towel.

2. In a small bowl, beat the eggs. In another small bowl, add the flour. Place the bread crumbs in a third small bowl.

3. Spray the air fryer basket with cooking oil.

4. Dip the pickle slices in the flour, then the egg, and then the bread crumbs.

5. Place the breaded pickle slices in the air fryer. It is okay to stack them. Spray them with cooking oil. Cook for 6 minutes.

6. Open the air fryer and flip the pickles. Cook for an additional 2 to 3 minutes, or until the pickles are crisp.

Substitution tip: Two egg whites can be substituted for the whole eggs to save on calories and fat.

Cooking tip: Check in on the pickles throughout the cooking process to monitor doneness and adjust cook time as necessary. The pickles will turn deep golden brown when crisp.

Per serving: Calories: 137; Total fat: 3g; Saturated fat: 1g; Cholesterol: 82mg; Sodium: 2372mg; Carbohydrates: 21g; Fiber: 4g; Protein: 7g

Spiced Nuts

FAST, FAMILY FAVORITE, VEGETARIAN, GLUTEN-FREE

BAKE: 300°F • PREP TIME: 5 MINUTES • COOK TIME: 15 MINUTES • SERVES 4

Full of healthy fats, these nuts make the perfect high-protein grab-and-go snack. They also make for a crowd-pleasing nosh at gatherings. (No one will suspect how easy they are to make!)

½ teaspoon cinnamon

½ teaspoon stevia

Pepper

1 cup nuts (walnuts, pecans, and almonds work well)

1 egg white

Cooking oil

1. In a small bowl, combine the cinnamon, stevia, and pepper to taste.
2. Place the nuts in another bowl with the egg white. Add the spices to the nuts.
3. Spray the air fryer basket with cooking oil.
4. Place the nuts in the air fryer. Spray them with cooking oil. Cook for 10 minutes.
5. Open the air fryer and shake the basket. Cook for an additional 3 to 4 minutes.
6. Serve warm.

Substitution tip: If you prefer sugar to stevia, you can substitute 1 teaspoon sugar for the stevia in this recipe.

Per serving: Calories: 210; Total fat: 18g; Saturated fat: 2g; Cholesterol: 0mg; Sodium: 237mg; Carbohydrates: 9g; Fiber: 3g; Protein: 7g

Pigs in a Blanket

FAST, FAMILY FAVORITE

FRY: 350°F • PREP TIME: 10 MINUTES • COOK TIME: 20 MINUTES
MAKES 16 PIGS IN A BLANKET (1 PIG IN A BLANKET = 1 SERVING)

When you're in a pinch and need to put a party appetizer out fast, this recipe delivers! These Pigs in a Blanket are a nostalgic classic that cooks up in minutes. This recipe also works for a quick lunch with salad on the side or as a midday snack.

1 (8-ounce) can crescent rolls or croissant biscuit rolls

16 cocktail franks or mini smoked hot dogs

Cooking oil

1. Separate the crescent roll dough into 8 triangles and place them on a flat work surface. Cut each triangle in half to make 16 triangles.

2. Dry the franks with a paper towel. Place 1 frank on the bottom of a triangle. This should be the widest part of the dough. Roll up the dough. Repeat for the remaining franks and triangles.

3. Spray the air fryer basket with cooking oil.

4. Place 8 pigs in a blanket in the air fryer. It is okay to stack them, but do not overcrowd the basket. Spray them with cooking oil. Cook for 8 minutes.

5. Remove the cooked pigs in a blanket from the air fryer, then repeat step 4 for the remaining 8 pigs in a blanket.

6. Cool before serving.

Substitution tip: You can use 6 standard-size sausages or hot dogs. Cut each into 2 or 3 smaller pieces to make 16 pieces total.

Per serving: Calories: 75; Total fat: 5g; Saturated fat: 2g; Cholesterol: 5mg; Sodium: 170mg; Carbohydrates: 6g; Fiber: 0g; Protein: 2g

Breaded Artichoke Hearts

FAST, VEGETARIAN

FRY: 380°F • PREP TIME: 15 MINUTES • COOK TIME: 10 MINUTES
MAKES 14 ARTICHOKE HEARTS (1 ARTICHOKE HEART = 1 SERVING)

The ingredients for this appetizer are normally in my pantry, so pulling it together takes very little effort. These warm and flaky panko-breaded artichoke hearts are designed to impress at dinner dates, parties, or events. No panko? Swap in regular bread crumbs for an equally delicious dish.

14 whole artichoke hearts packed in water

1 egg

½ cup all-purpose flour

⅓ cup panko bread crumbs

1 teaspoon Italian seasoning

Cooking oil

1. Squeeze excess water from the artichoke hearts and place them on paper towels to dry.
2. In a small bowl, beat the egg. In another small bowl, place the flour. In a third small bowl, combine the bread crumbs and Italian seasoning, and stir.
3. Spray the air fryer basket with cooking oil.
4. Dip the artichoke hearts in the flour, then the egg, and then the bread crumb mixture.
5. Place the breaded artichoke hearts in the air fryer. It is okay to stack them. Spray them with cooking oil. Cook for 4 minutes.
6. Open the air fryer and flip the artichoke hearts. I recommend flipping instead of shaking because the hearts are small, and this will help keep the breading intact. Cook for an additional 4 minutes, or until the artichoke hearts have browned and are crisp.
7. Cool before serving.

Ingredient tip: You can create your own Italian seasoning by combining ¼ teaspoon each of thyme, oregano, basil, and red pepper flakes.

Cooking tip: Check in on the artichokes throughout the cooking process to monitor doneness and adjust cook time as necessary. The artichokes will turn deep golden brown when crisp.

Per serving: Calories: 54; Total fat: 1g; Saturated fat: 0g; Cholesterol: 12mg; Sodium: 248mg; Carbohydrates: 9g; Fiber: 1g; Protein: 3g

Crunchy Pork Egg Rolls

FAST, FAMILY FAVORITE

FRY: 400°F • PREP TIME: 15 MINUTES • COOK TIME: 15 MINUTES
MAKES 12 EGG ROLLS (1 EGG ROLL = 1 SERVING)

Air-fried egg rolls far surpass the typical freebies Chinese restaurants throw in with your takeout. These rolls are packed with tasty ground pork, fresh vegetables, and bold sauces to produce mouthwatering flavor without the grease. A basting brush can help you assemble your egg rolls.

Cooking oil

2 garlic cloves, minced

1 teaspoon sesame oil

¼ cup soy sauce

2 teaspoons grated fresh ginger

12 ounces ground pork

½ cabbage, shredded (2 cups)

4 scallions, green parts (white parts optional), chopped

24 egg roll wrappers

1. Spray a skillet with cooking oil and place over medium-high heat. Add the garlic. Cook for 1 minute, until fragrant.

2. Add the ground pork to the skillet. Using a spoon, break the pork into smaller chunks.

3. In a small bowl, combine the sesame oil, soy sauce, and ginger. Mix well to combine.

4. Add the sauce to the skillet. Stir to combine. Continue cooking for 5 minutes, until the pork is browned.

5. When the pork has browned, add the cabbage and scallions. Mix well.

6. Transfer the pork mixture to a large bowl.

7. Lay the egg roll wrappers on a flat surface. Dip a basting brush in water and glaze each of the egg roll wrappers along the edges with the wet brush. This will soften the dough and make it easier to roll.

8. Stack 2 egg roll wrappers (it works best if you double-wrap the egg rolls). Scoop 1 to 2 tablespoons of the pork mixture onto the center.

9. Roll one long side of the wrappers up over the filling. Press firmly on the area with the filling, tucking it in lightly to secure it in place. Next, fold in the left and right sides.

10. Continue rolling to close. Use the basting brush to wet the seam and seal the egg roll.

11. Place the egg rolls in the basket of the air fryer. It is okay to stack them. Spray them with cooking oil. Cook for 8 minutes.

12. Flip the egg rolls. Cook for an additional 4 minutes.

13. Cool before serving.

Substitution tip: Grated fresh ginger, or ginger sold in jars in the produce section of the grocery store, works best in this recipe, but you can use 1 teaspoon ground ginger, which can be found in the spice aisle.

Ingredient tip: I think the soy sauce provides enough salt and seasoning for this recipe. Taste your cooked pork mixture prior to stuffing the egg rolls to determine if you need to add any salt.

Prep tip: I like to purchase cabbage preshredded, which helps save time.

Cooking tip: When you open the air fryer at 8 minutes to flip the egg rolls, evaluate how much longer you think they will need to cook. Touch them with a knife or fork to determine if they are crunchy enough.

Per serving: Calories: 244; Total fat: 4g; Saturated fat: 1g; Cholesterol: 27mg; Sodium: 683mg; Carbohydrates: 39g; Fiber: 2g; Protein: 12g

Spinach and Artichoke Dip Wontons

VEGETARIAN

FRY: 375°F • PREP TIME: 15 MINUTES • COOK TIME: 40 MINUTES
MAKES 20 WONTONS (2 WONTONS = 1 SERVING)

When I first tested this recipe, I thought I had died and gone to heaven. These are perfect for parties. A great improvement over artichoke dip in a bread bowl, this rich-tasting appetizer served up in an elegant little package will impress your guests. Better make a double batch because these will *not* last.

6 ounces cream cheese

¼ cup sour cream

¼ cup shredded Parmesan cheese

¼ cup shredded mozzarella cheese

5 ounces frozen chopped spinach, thawed and drained

6 ounces marinated artichoke hearts, drained

2 garlic cloves, chopped

Salt

Pepper

20 wonton wrappers

Cooking oil

1. In a small, microwave-safe bowl, heat the cream cheese in the microwave for 20 seconds to soften.

2. In a medium bowl, combine the cream cheese, sour cream, Parmesan, mozzarella, spinach, artichoke hearts, garlic, and salt and pepper to taste. Stir to mix well.

3. Lay out the wonton wrappers on a work surface. A clean table or large cutting board works well.

4. Scoop 1½ teaspoons of the artichoke mixture onto each wrapper. Be careful not to overfill.

5. Fold each wrapper diagonally to form a triangle. Bring the two bottom corners up toward each other. Do not close the wrapper yet. Bring up the two open sides and push out any air. Squeeze the open edges together to seal.

6. Place the wontons in the air fryer basket and cook in batches, or stack (see Air fryer cooking tip). Spray the wontons with cooking oil. Cook for 10 minutes.

7. Remove the basket and flip the wontons. Return to the air fryer and cook for an additional 5 to 8 minutes, until the wontons have reached your desired level of golden-brown crispiness.

8. If cooking in batches, remove the cooked wontons from the air fryer, then repeat steps 6 and 7 for the remaining wontons.

9. Cool before serving.

Substitution tip: I prefer to use reduced-fat cream cheese and sour cream. It helps keep the calories and fat content low, making it a bit friendlier to my waistline—and the difference in taste is imperceptible.

Cooking tip: Check in on the wontons throughout the cooking process to ensure they do not overheat. The wontons have finished cooking when the color has reached a light golden brown. If the wontons overheat, the filling may leak.

Air fryer cooking tip: You can choose to stack the wontons throughout the air fryer or cook them in separate batches. The total cook time indicated (40 minutes) is for two batches. While stacking them is quicker, preparing the wontons in batches works best. If you stack them, you may have a few that are really soft and break apart when you try to flip them over.

Per serving: Calories: 166; Total fat: 7g; Saturated fat: 3g; Cholesterol: 14mg; Sodium: 345mg; Carbohydrates: 21g; Fiber: 1g; Protein: 5g

Loaded Disco Fries

FAST, FAMILY FAVORITE

FRY: 400°F • PREP TIME: 5 MINUTES • COOK TIME: 25 MINUTES • SERVES 5

These cheese fries define *decadent*. Inspired by classic Canadian poutine (pronounced "poo-TEEN"), Loaded Disco Fries are crispy steak fries piled with gooey mozzarella cheese and rich brown gravy. Making them in the air fryer dramatically cuts down on the fat.

1 (28-ounce) bag frozen steak fries

Cooking oil

Salt

Pepper

½ cup beef gravy

1 cup shredded mozzarella cheese

2 scallions, green parts only, chopped

1. Place the frozen steak fries in the air fryer. Cook for 10 minutes.

2. Open the air fryer and shake the basket. Spray the fries with cooking oil. Sprinkle with salt and pepper to taste. Cook for an additional 8 minutes.

3. Pour the beef gravy into a medium, microwave-safe bowl. Microwave for 30 seconds, or until the gravy is warm.

4. Open the air fryer and sprinkle the fries with the cheese. Cook for an additional 2 minutes, until the cheese is melted.

5. Transfer the fries to a serving dish. Drizzle the fries with gravy and sprinkle the scallions on top for a green garnish. Serve.

Substitution tip: Any type of gravy will work for this recipe.

Per serving: Calories: 291; Total fat: 11g; Saturated fat: 4g; Cholesterol: 18mg; Sodium: 774mg; Carbohydrates: 39g; Fiber: 3g; Protein: 1g

---

AREN'T YOU GLAD YOU DIDN'T DEEP-FRY?

You save more than 50 grams of fat per serving preparing this dish in the air fryer instead of ordering it at a restaurant!

Apple Chips

FAST, FAMILY FAVORITE, VEGETARIAN, GLUTEN-FREE

BAKE: 350°F • PREP TIME: 5 MINUTES • COOK TIME: 10 MINUTES • SERVES 4

Ditch your roll-ups and gummy snacks for this healthy treat made from real fruit. Processed snacks are often loaded with high-fructose corn syrup. Instead, take a mere 15 minutes and use your air fryer to make this wholesome recipe; it's perfect for hungry little ones.

4 medium apples (any type will work), cored

¼ teaspoon cinnamon

¼ teaspoon nutmeg

1. Cut the apples into ⅓-inch-thick slices. Thin slices yield crunchy chips.
2. Place the apple slices in a large bowl. Sprinkle the cinnamon and nutmeg onto the apple slices.
3. Transfer the apple chips to the air fryer. It is okay to stack them. Cook for 6 minutes.
4. Open the air fryer and shake the basket. Cook for an additional 4 minutes, or until crunchy.
5. Cool before serving.

Prep tip: Thickly sliced apples will turn out mushy. Try to slice them as thin as possible. Using a mandoline will help.

Cooking tips:

➢ Don't spray with cooking oil—if you do, the chips will taste burnt.

➢ Check in on the apples when you shake them. Taste one and use your judgment as to how much additional cooking time is needed.

Per serving: Calories: 117; Total fat: 1g; Saturated fat: 0g; Cholesterol: 0mg; Sodium: 2mg; Carbohydrates: 31g; Fiber: 6g; Protein: 1g

Sweet Potato Fries

FAMILY FAVORITE, VEGETARIAN, GLUTEN-FREE

FRY: 380°F • PREP TIME: 10 MINUTES, PLUS 1 HOUR TO SOAK
COOK TIME: 25 MINUTES • SERVES 4

For this recipe, you need a sealable plastic bag to coat the fries in cornstarch. Sweet potato fries can be tough to prepare from scratch. But when you fully coat the sweet potatoes, your end result delivers the crunchy mouthfeel you crave.

2 large sweet
potatoes, peeled

1½ tablespoons
cornstarch

1 tablespoon canola oil

1 tablespoon extra-virgin
olive oil

1 teaspoon paprika

1 teaspoon garlic powder

Salt

Pepper

1. Cut the potatoes lengthwise to create fries. Place them in a large bowl with cold water. Allow them to soak in the water for 1 hour.

2. Drain the sweet potatoes and pat dry with paper towels or napkins.

3. Place the fries in a sealable plastic bag and add the cornstarch. Seal the bag and shake to evenly coat the fries.

4. Place the fries in a large bowl and coat with the canola oil and olive oil. Add the paprika, garlic powder, and salt and pepper to taste.

5. Transfer the fries to the air fryer basket. It is okay to stack the fries, but do not overcrowd the basket. Cook for 10 minutes.

6. Open the air fryer and shake the basket. Cook for an additional 10 to 15 minutes, until the fries are crisp.

7. Cool before serving.

Cooking tip: Test doneness by poking the fries with a knife or fork. The surface should feel hard.

Per serving: Calories: 121; Total fat: 7g; Saturated fat: 1g; Cholesterol: 0mg; Sodium: 75mg; Carbohydrates: 16g; Fiber: 2g; Protein: 1g

Kale Chips

FAST, VEGETARIAN, GLUTEN-FREE

Kale is low in calories and fat but high in fiber. These superfood chips provide a nutritious snack. These are best enjoyed shortly after they come out of your air fryer, but storing the chips in a paper bag will help them retain their crunch the next day.

1 bunch fresh kale, ribs removed, chopped into large pieces

1 tablespoon extra-virgin olive oil

Salt

Pepper

1. In a large bowl, combine the kale and olive oil, and season with salt and pepper. Mix well to ensure the kale is fully coated.

2. Place the kale in the air fryer basket. Cook for 5 minutes.

3. Open the air fryer and shake the basket. Cook for an additional 5 minutes.

4. Cool before serving.

Variation tip: Feel free to add your favorite seasonings to the mix (e.g., garlic powder, onion powder, red pepper flakes).

Per serving: Calories: 80; Total fat: 4g; Saturated fat: 1g; Cholesterol: 0mg; Sodium: 82mg; Carbohydrates: 11g; Fiber: 2g; Protein: 3g

Jalapeño Cheese Balls

FAMILY FAVORITE, VEGETARIAN

FRY: 400°F • PREP TIME: 15 MINUTES, PLUS 15 MINUTES TO CHILL
COOK TIME: 15 MINUTES • MAKES 12 CHEESE BALLS (1 CHEESE BALL = 1 SERVING)

A winning variation on a large cheese ball dip, these individual spicy cheese bites serve up bold flavors at a backyard bash or your next tailgate. (Think: No more double-dipping!) With the air fryer, you can prep in advance and cook up a batch in minutes, leaving more time for socializing with your guests.

4 ounces cream cheese

⅓ cup shredded mozzarella cheese

⅓ cup shredded Cheddar cheese

2 jalapeños, finely chopped

½ cup bread crumbs

2 eggs

½ cup all-purpose flour

Salt

Pepper

Cooking oil

1. In a medium bowl, combine the cream cheese, mozzarella, Cheddar, and jalapeños. Mix well.

2. Form the cheese mixture into balls about an inch thick. Using a small ice cream scoop works well.

3. Arrange the cheese balls on a sheet pan and place in the freezer for 15 minutes. This will help the cheese balls maintain their shape while frying.

4. Spray the air fryer basket with cooking oil.

5. Place the bread crumbs in a small bowl. In another small bowl, beat the eggs. In a third small bowl, combine the flour with salt and pepper to taste, and mix well.

6. Remove the cheese balls from the freezer. Dip the cheese balls in the flour, then the eggs, and then the bread crumbs.

7. Place the cheese balls in the air fryer. (It is okay to stack them.) Spray with cooking oil. Cook for 8 minutes.

8. Open the air fryer and flip the cheese balls. I recommend flipping them instead of shaking so the balls maintain their form. Cook an additional 4 minutes.

9. Cool before serving.

Substitution tip: Seasoned bread crumbs work well with this recipe. Reduced-fat cheeses, such as cream cheese, mozzarella, and Cheddar, will make the recipe lighter and healthier.

Prep tip: I recommend wearing disposable gloves while handling the jalapeños. Or wash your hands immediately after working with them, and don't rub your eyes (this burns).

Cooking tip: Check in on the cheese balls throughout the cooking process to monitor doneness and adjust cook time as necessary. The cheese balls will turn deep golden brown when crisp.

Per serving: Calories: 96; Total fat: 6g; Saturated fat: 3g; Cholesterol: 41mg; Sodium: 107mg; Carbohydrates: 8g; Fiber: 0g; Protein: 4g

Salsa and Cheese Stuffed Mushrooms

FAST, VEGETARIAN, GLUTEN-FREE

BAKE: 370°F • PREP TIME: 10 MINUTES • COOK TIME: 10 MINUTES • SERVES 5

This low-carb dish is perfect for vegetarian Taco Tuesday nights! Leave the taco shell and carbs behind for this savory delicacy. Your air fryer will transform these mushrooms into decadent bites dripping with melted cheese. These mushrooms also work wonderfully as a side dish.

8 ounces large portobello mushrooms

⅓ cup salsa

½ cup shredded Cheddar cheese

Cooking oil

1. Cut the stem out of the mushrooms: First, chop off the end of the stem, and then make a circular cut around the area where the stem was. Continue to cut until you have removed the rest of the stem.

2. Stuff the mushrooms with the salsa. Sprinkle the shredded cheese on top.

3. Place the mushrooms in the air fryer. Cook for 8 minutes.

4. Cool before serving.

Substitution tip: Feel free to substitute your favorite type of easy-melting cheese for this recipe. Pepper Jack or a Mexican cheese blend pairs well with the salsa.

Ingredient tip: When you grate your own cheese, it melts better than cheese that you buy preshredded in a bag.

Per serving: Calories: 64; Total fat: 4g; Saturated fat: 2g; Cholesterol: 12mg; Sodium: 174mg; Carbohydrates: 3g; Fiber: 0g; Protein: 4g

Fried Olives

FAST, FAMILY FAVORITE, VEGETARIAN

FRY: 400°F • PREP TIME: 15 MINUTES • COOK TIME: 10 MINUTES • SERVES 4

Assembled in minutes with everyday items you likely have stocked in your pantry, fried olives make a unique appetizer for gatherings. The olives pair well with assorted cheese and fruit, offsetting their chewy and sweet attributes with a savory and crunchy punch.

1 (5½-ounce) jar pitted green olives

½ cup all-purpose flour

Salt

Pepper

½ cup bread crumbs

1 egg

Cooking oil

1. Remove the olives from the jar and dry thoroughly with paper towels.

2. In a small bowl, combine the flour with salt and pepper to taste. Place the bread crumbs in another small bowl. In a third small bowl, beat the egg.

3. Spray the air fryer basket with cooking oil.

4. Dip the olives in the flour, then the egg, and then the bread crumbs.

5. Place the breaded olives in the air fryer. It is okay to stack them. Spray the olives with cooking oil. Cook for 6 minutes.

6. Open the air fryer. Flip the olives. Because olives are small, I prefer to flip them instead of shaking to maintain the breading.

7. Cook for an additional 2 minutes, or until brown and crisp.

8. Cool before serving.

Substitution tip: Seasoned bread crumbs work well with this recipe.

Cooking tip: Check in on the olives throughout the cooking process to monitor doneness.

Per serving: Calories: 165; Total fat: 5g; Saturated fat: 1g; Cholesterol: 41mg; Sodium: 828mg; Carbohydrates: 24g; Fiber: 4g; Protein: 5g

Potato Skin Bites

FAMILY FAVORITE, GLUTEN-FREE

FRY: 400°F • PREP TIME: 15 MINUTES • COOK TIME: 20 MINUTES
MAKES 25 BITES (1 BITE = 1 SERVING)

These bites have the appeal of a loaded baked potato but are trimmed down and served as an appetizer. Perfect for parties and events, they also work as a kid-friendly snack. Feeling decadent? Add a dollop each of sour cream and salsa for extra layers of flavor.

4 slices bacon

4 large russet potatoes

1 tablespoon extra-virgin olive oil

1 teaspoon paprika

Salt

Pepper

1 cup shredded Cheddar cheese

2 teaspoons chopped chives

2 teaspoons chopped scallions, green parts (white parts optional)

1. In a skillet over medium-high heat, cook the bacon for about 5 to 7 minutes, flipping to evenly crisp. Drain on paper towels, crumble, and set aside.

2. Cut the potatoes into ½-inch-thick rounds. Place the potato rounds in a large bowl with the olive oil and paprika, and season with salt and pepper to taste. Toss to fully coat.

3. Place the potatoes in the air fryer basket. It is okay stack them, but do not overcrowd the basket. You may need to cook the potatoes in two batches. Cook for 10 minutes.

4. Open the air fryer and shake the basket. Cook for an additional 5 to 8 minutes, until the potato skin bites are soft in the middle and crisp along the edges.

5. Transfer the potato skin bites to a serving dish. Top with the shredded cheese, crumbled bacon, chives, and scallions. Serve.

Cooking tip: Poke the center of a potato skin bite to monitor doneness. The center should be soft.

Per serving: Calories: 81; Total fat: 3g; Saturated fat: 2g; Cholesterol: 8mg; Sodium: 110mg; Carbohydrates: 9g; Fiber: 2g; Protein: 3g

Buffalo Breaded Cauliflower Bites

FAMILY FAVORITE, VEGETARIAN

FRY: 370°F • PREP TIME: 10 MINUTES • COOK TIME: 25 MINUTES • SERVES 4

Craving that signature Buffalo flavor, but trying to eat more veggies? If so, this is the recipe for you. Breaded cauliflower makes a surprisingly solid vegetarian substitute for Buffalo chicken wings. As a bonus, you benefit from cauliflower's nutrient-dense goodness.

1 cup all-purpose flour

1 cup water

1 teaspoon garlic powder

1 large head cauliflower, cut into florets (4 cups)

Cooking oil

⅓ cup Frank's RedHot Buffalo Wings sauce

1. In a large bowl, combine the flour, water, and garlic powder. Mix well. The mixture should resemble pancake batter.

2. Add the cauliflower to the batter and stir to coat. Transfer the cauliflower to another large bowl to drain the excess batter.

3. Spray the air fryer with cooking oil.

4. Transfer the cauliflower to the air fryer. Do not stack. Cook in batches. Spray the cauliflower with cooking oil. Cook for 6 minutes.

5. Open the air fryer and transfer the cauliflower to a large bowl. Drizzle with the Buffalo sauce. Mix well.

6. Return the cauliflower to the air fryer. Cook for an additional 6 minutes, or until crisp.

7. Remove the cooked cauliflower from the air fryer, then repeat steps 4 through 6 for the remaining cauliflower batches.

8. Cool before serving.

Substitution tip: If Frank's RedHot Buffalo Wings Sauce is not available in your local grocery store, use any Buffalo sauce you can easily get your hands on, or make your own with regular Frank's RedHot (see Substitution tip on page 103).

Per serving: Calories: 170; Total fat: 1g; Saturated fat: 0g; Cholesterol: 0mg; Sodium: 95mg; Carbohydrates: 36g; Fiber: 6g; Protein: 8g

Crispy Brussels Sprouts, page 71

CHAPTER 5

Vegetables and Sides

Parmesan Garlic Breaded Cauliflower

VEGETARIAN

BAKE: 370°F • PREP TIME: 10 MINUTES • COOK TIME: 25 MINUTES • SERVES 4

Eating veggies can be an enjoyable experience—especially when Parmesan cheese is involved! This cauliflower dish comes together quickly. The recipe follows the standard three-step breading process using flour, eggs, and bread crumbs.

2 eggs

⅓ cup all-purpose flour

½ cup Italian seasoned bread crumbs

1 teaspoon garlic powder

2 tablespoons grated Parmesan cheese

Salt

Pepper

1 large head cauliflower, cut into florets (4 cups)

Cooking oil

1. In a small bowl, beat the eggs. Place the flour in another bowl and the bread crumbs in a third bowl.

2. To the bowl of bread crumbs, add the garlic powder, Parmesan cheese, and salt and pepper to taste. Stir to combine.

3. Spray the air fryer basket with cooking oil.

4. Dip the cauliflower florets in the flour, then the egg, and then the bread crumb mixture.

5. Place the cauliflower in the air fryer basket. Do not stack. Cook in batches. Spray the cauliflower with cooking oil. Cook for 6 minutes.

6. Open the air fryer and shake the basket. Cook for an additional 4 to 6 minutes, or until the cauliflower has browned slightly.

7. Remove the cooked cauliflower from the air fryer, then repeat steps 5 and 6 with the remaining cauliflower.

8. Cool before serving.

Substitution tip: Opt for egg whites instead of whole eggs to save on calories and fat.

Per serving: Calories: 194; Total fat: 4g; Saturated fat: 2g; Cholesterol: 84mg; Sodium: 429mg; Carbohydrates: 30g; Fiber: 6g; Protein: 11g

Crispy Brussels Sprouts

FAST, VEGETARIAN, GLUTEN-FREE

BAKE: 380°F • PREP TIME: 5 MINUTES • COOK TIME: 15 MINUTES • SERVES 4

The air fryer cooks Brussels sprouts in a fraction of the time they'd cook in the oven. The result? Brussels sprouts that are crispy on the outside and roasted to perfection on the inside. Slightly bitter, Brussels sprouts taste somewhat like cabbage and pair wonderfully with roasted chicken or fish. Or add the mustard aioli and serve these as a delicious appetizer.

For the Brussels sprouts

1 pound Brussels sprouts, halved (2 cups)

1 teaspoon garlic powder

Salt

Pepper

Cooking oil

For the mustard aioli

½ cup mayonnaise

½ tablespoon olive oil

1 tablespoon Dijon mustard

1 teaspoon minced garlic

Salt

Pepper

1 tablespoon chopped parsley

To make the Brussels sprouts

1. In a large bowl, combine the Brussels sprouts with the garlic powder. Season with salt and pepper to taste.

2. Place the Brussels sprouts in the air fryer. Spray them with cooking oil. Cook for 6 minutes.

3. Open the air fryer and shake the basket. Cook for an additional 6 to 7 minutes, until the Brussels sprouts have turned slightly brown.

To make the mustard aioli

1. While the Brussels sprouts are cooking, combine the mayonnaise, olive oil, mustard, and garlic in a small bowl, adding salt and pepper to taste. Mix well until fully combined. Sprinkle with parsley to garnish.

2. Cool the Brussels sprouts and serve alongside the aioli.

Variation tip: If you have balsamic vinegar in your pantry, you can drizzle it over your Brussels sprouts either before or after cooking to add an additional layer of flavor to your dish.

Prep tip: To save even more time, look for pretrimmed, bagged Brussels sprouts at your grocery store.

Per serving (includes 2 tablespoons of aioli): Calories: 172; Total fat: 11g; Saturated fat: 2g; Cholesterol: 8mg; Sodium: 267mg; Carbohydrates: 18g; Fiber: 5g; Protein: 4g

Twice-Baked Potatoes

FAMILY FAVORITE, GLUTEN-FREE

BAKE: 400°F • PREP TIME: 15 MINUTES • COOK TIME: 50 MINUTES
MAKES 8 POTATO HALVES (1 POTATO HALF = 1 SERVING)

Baked potatoes usually take more than an hour to prepare in the oven. Using the air fryer saves 20 minutes! A twice-baked potato is first baked to soften the potato, then half of the inside is removed to create a mashed potato stuffing that goes back into the potato shell. The potato is baked again to create a cheesy, crunchy topping with a creamy interior.

4 large russet potatoes

4 slices bacon

2 tablespoons butter

½ cup milk

1 teaspoon garlic powder

Salt

Pepper

2 scallions, green
   parts (white parts
   optional), chopped

2 tablespoons sour cream

1¼ cups shredded
   Cheddar cheese, divided

1. Using a fork, poke three holes into the top of each potato.

2. Place the potatoes in the air fryer. Cook for 40 minutes.

3. Meanwhile, in a skillet over medium-high heat, cook the bacon for about 5 to 7 minutes, flipping to evenly crisp. Drain on paper towels, crumble, and set aside.

4. Remove the cooked potatoes from the air fryer and allow them to cool for 10 minutes.

5. While the potatoes cool, heat a saucepan over medium-high heat. Add the butter and milk. Stir. Allow the mixture to cook for 2 to 3 minutes, until the butter has melted.

6. Halve each of the potatoes lengthwise. Scoop half of the flesh out of the middle of each potato half, leaving the flesh on the surrounding edges. This will hold the potato together when you stuff it.

7. Place the potato flesh in a large bowl and mash with a potato masher. Add the warm butter and milk mixture and stir to combine. Season with the garlic powder and salt and pepper to taste.

8. Add the cooked bacon, scallions, sour cream, and 1 cup of Cheddar cheese. Stir to combine.

9. Stuff each potato half with 1 to 2 tablespoons of the mashed potato mixture. Sprinkle the remaining ¼ cup of Cheddar cheese on top of the potato halves.

10. Place 4 potato halves in the air fryer. Do not stack. Cook for 2 to 3 minutes, or until the cheese has melted.

11. Remove the cooked potatoes from the air fryer, then repeat step 10 for the remaining 4 potato halves.

12. Cool before serving.

Variation tip: Feel free to add your favorite baked potato toppings. Paprika, ranch dressing, and chives work well. Omit the bacon for a vegetarian option.

Cooking tip: When first baking the potatoes, poke the inside with a fork or knife to monitor doneness. The inside of the potatoes should be soft.

Per serving: Calories: 292; Total fat: 14g; Saturated fat: 8g; Cholesterol: 39mg; Sodium: 389mg; Carbohydrates: 31g; Fiber: 5g; Protein: 12g

Crunchy Green Beans

FAST, VEGETARIAN, GLUTEN-FREE

These green beans make a great low-carb side dish to pair with chicken, pork, or beef. The beans are not breaded, but they are crunchy and loaded with flavor.

1½ pounds green beans, trimmed

1 tablespoon extra-virgin olive oil

1 teaspoon garlic powder

Salt

Pepper

1. In a large bowl, drizzle the green beans with the olive oil. Sprinkle with the garlic powder and salt and pepper to taste. Mix well.

2. Transfer the green beans to the air fryer basket. Cook for 4 minutes.

3. Open the air fryer and shake the basket. Cook for an additional 3 to 4 minutes, until the green beans have turned slightly brown.

4. Cool before serving.

Cooking tip: If you prefer al dente green beans, 7 to 8 minutes of cooking time is optimal. If you prefer softer green beans, cook for 10 minutes or more, and open the air fryer frequently to monitor doneness.

Per serving: Calories: 83; Total fat: 4g; Saturated fat: 1g; Cholesterol: 0mg; Sodium: 49mg; Carbohydrates: 12g; Fiber: 6g; Protein: 3g

Garlic-Roasted Red Potatoes

FAST, FAMILY FAVORITE, VEGETARIAN, GLUTEN-FREE

BAKE: 370°F • PREP TIME: 5 MINUTES • COOK TIME: 20 MINUTES • SERVES 4

These roasted red potatoes pair well with steak dinners. You first need to marinate the potatoes using a sealed plastic bag. Then dump the potatoes into the air fryer. No heavy lifting is required!

6 red potatoes, cut into 1-inch cubes

3 garlic cloves, minced

Salt

Pepper

1 teaspoon chopped chives

1 tablespoon extra-virgin olive oil

1. In a sealable plastic bag, combine the potatoes, garlic, salt and pepper to taste, chives, and olive oil. Seal the bag and shake to coat the potatoes.

2. Transfer the potatoes to the air fryer. Cook for 10 minutes.

3. Open the air fryer and shake the basket. Cook for an additional 10 minutes.

4. Cool before serving.

Cooking tip: Poke the inside of potatoes with a fork or knife to monitor doneness. The inside of the potatoes should be soft.

Per serving: Calories: 257; Total fat: 4g; Saturated fat: 1g; Cholesterol: 0mg; Sodium: 58mg; Carbohydrates: 52g; Fiber: 6g; Protein: 6g

Cauliflower Fried Rice

VEGETARIAN

FRY: 375°F • PREP TIME: 25 MINUTES • COOK TIME: 20 MINUTES • SERVES 5

This low-carb fried rice variation has enough veggies for a main dish but also works well as a side. My go-to is the riced cauliflower from Trader Joe's. You can find it in the frozen vegetables section. You can also make your own riced cauliflower, but purchasing it ready-made just makes the process easier. You will need a barrel accessory pan for this recipe.

2½ cups riced cauliflower
(1 head cauliflower if
making your own)

2 teaspoons sesame
oil, divided

1 medium green bell
pepper, chopped

1 cup peas

1 cup diced carrots

½ cup chopped onion

Salt

Pepper

1 tablespoon soy sauce

2 medium eggs, scrambled

1. If you choose to make your own riced cauliflower, grate the head of cauliflower using the medium-size holes of a cheese grater. Or you can cut the head of cauliflower into florets and pulse in a food processer until it has the appearance of rice.

2. Coat the bottom of a barrel pan with 1 teaspoon of sesame oil.

3. In a large bowl, combine the riced cauliflower, green bell pepper, peas, carrots, and onion. Drizzle the remaining 1 teaspoon of sesame oil over the vegetables and stir. Add salt and pepper to taste.

4. Transfer the mixture to the barrel pan. Cook for 10 minutes.

5. Remove the barrel pan. Drizzle the soy sauce all over and add the scrambled eggs. Stir to combine.

6. Serve warm.

Substitution tip: Sesame oil is used because it provides Asian flavor. Canola, olive, or grapeseed oil can be substituted, but it will not provide the same taste.

Variation tip: To make this recipe gluten-free, replace with soy sauce with tamari. You can find it in the same aisle as soy sauce in the grocery store. Be sure to check the label.

Per serving: Calories: 81; Total fat: 4g; Saturated fat: 1g; Cholesterol: 65mg; Sodium: 280mg; Carbohydrates: 9g; Fiber: 4g; Protein: 5g

Vegetable Medley

FAST, VEGETARIAN, GLUTEN-FREE

This colorful medley will brighten any table and pairs wonderfully with main dishes. This dish delivers amazing flavor with perfect texture. Feel free to get creative with your own favorite veggies, seasonings, and spices to add more pizzazz.

1 head broccoli, chopped (about 2 cups)

2 medium carrots, cut into 1-inch pieces

Salt

Pepper

Cooking oil

1 zucchini, cut into 1-inch chunks

1 medium red bell pepper, seeded and thinly sliced

1. In a large bowl, combine the broccoli and carrots. Season with salt and pepper to taste. Spray with cooking oil.

2. Transfer the broccoli and carrots to the air fryer basket. Cook for 6 minutes.

3. Place the zucchini and red pepper in the bowl. Season with salt and pepper to taste. Spray with cooking oil.

4. Add the zucchini and red pepper to the broccoli and carrots in the air fryer basket. Cook for 6 minutes.

5. Cool before serving.

Per serving: Calories: 47; Total fat: 1g; Saturated fat: 0g; Cholesterol: 0mg; Sodium: 80mg; Carbohydrates: 10g; Fiber: 3g; Protein: 2g

Fried Breaded Okra

FAST, FAMILY FAVORITE, VEGETARIAN

FRY: 380°F • PREP TIME: 15 MINUTES • COOK TIME: 10 MINUTES • SERVES 4

Fried okra is a traditional Southern dish. I love okra when it is prepared in gumbo and stews, but breaded and fried, it tastes extra decadent!

1½ cups okra, cut into ¼-inch pieces

3 tablespoons buttermilk

2 tablespoons all-purpose flour

2 tablespoons cornmeal

Salt

Pepper

Cooking oil

1. Make sure the okra pieces are dry, using paper towels if needed.
2. Pour the buttermilk into a small bowl. In another small bowl, combine the flour and cornmeal, and season with salt and pepper to taste.
3. Spray the air fryer basket with cooking oil.
4. Dip the okra in the buttermilk, then the flour and cornmeal.
5. Place the okra in the air fryer basket. It is okay to stack it. Spray the okra with cooking oil. Cook for 5 minutes.
6. Open the air fryer and shake the basket. Cook for an additional 5 minutes, or until the okra is crisp.
7. Cool before serving.

AREN'T YOU GLAD YOU DIDN'T DEEP-FRY?

The air fryer saves 10 grams of fat per serving in comparison to deep-fried okra.

Cooking tip: Check in on the okra throughout the cooking process to monitor doneness and adjust cook time as necessary. The okra will turn deep golden brown when crisp.

Per serving: Calories: 49; Total fat: 1g; Saturated Fat: 0g; Cholesterol: 0mg; Sodium: 55mg; Carbohydrates: 9g; Fiber: 2g; Protein: 2g

Eggplant Parmesan

FAMILY FAVORITE, VEGETARIAN

FRY: 400°F • PREP TIME: 15 MINUTES • COOK TIME: 20 MINUTES • SERVES 4

Here is a yummy option for Meatless Monday! Eggplant Parmesan is an Italian dish featuring eggplant slathered in marinara and melted cheese, served over pasta. When cooked in the air fryer, this veggie classic stays crunchy on the outside and tender on the inside.

1 medium eggplant, peeled

2 eggs

½ cup all-purpose flour

¾ cup Italian bread crumbs

2 tablespoons grated Parmesan cheese

Salt

Pepper

¾ cup marinara sauce

½ cup shredded Parmesan cheese

½ cup shredded mozzarella cheese

1. Cut the eggplant into ½-inch-thick rounds. Blot the eggplant with paper towels to dry completely. You can also sprinkle with a teaspoon of salt to sweat out the moisture.

2. In a small bowl, beat the eggs. Place the flour in another small bowl. In a third small bowl, combine the bread crumbs, grated Parmesan cheese, and salt and pepper to taste, and mix well.

3. Spray the air fryer basket with cooking oil.

4. Dip each eggplant round in the flour, then the eggs, and then the bread crumb mixture.

5. Place the eggplant rounds in the air fryer basket. Do not stack. Cook in batches. Spray the eggplant with cooking oil. Cook for 7 minutes.

6. Open the air fryer. Top each of the rounds with 1 teaspoon of marinara sauce and ½ tablespoon each of shredded Parmesan and mozzarella cheese. Cook for an additional 2 to 3 minutes, until the cheese has melted.

7. Remove the cooked eggplant from the air fryer, then repeat steps 5 and 6 for the remaining eggplant.

8. Cool before serving.

Ingredient tip: Fresh Parmesan cheese that you grate and shred yourself melts better than pregrated and preshredded options. If you want to use fresh mozzarella, top each piece of eggplant with a thinly sliced round and monitor the cooking time closely to make sure the cheese fully melts.

Per serving: Calories: 310; Total fat: 9g; Saturated fat: 4g; Cholesterol: 97mg; Sodium: 844mg; Carbohydrates: 42g; Fiber: 7g; Protein: 16g

Fried Green Tomatoes

FAMILY FAVORITE, VEGETARIAN

FRY: 400°F • PREP TIME: 15 MINUTES • COOK TIME: 30 MINUTES • SERVES 4

Repopularized in the early '90s by the movie of the same name, fried green tomatoes are a hallmark of Southern cuisine. In the air fryer, these battered unripe tomatoes transform into a mouthwatering treat—crispy on the outside and soft on the inside. Serve them as a side dish with your favorite main or as an appetizer with a side of ranch dip.

2 green tomatoes

2 eggs

½ cup all-purpose flour

½ cup yellow cornmeal

½ cup panko bread crumbs

1 teaspoon garlic powder

Salt

Pepper

Cooking oil

1. Cut the tomatoes into ½-inch-thick rounds.

2. In a small bowl, beat the eggs. In another small bowl, place the flour. In a third small bowl, combine the yellow cornmeal and panko bread crumbs, and season with the garlic powder and salt and pepper to taste. Mix well to combine.

3. Spray the air fryer basket with cooking oil.

4. Dip each tomato slice in the flour, then the egg, and then the cornmeal and bread crumb mixture.

5. Place the tomato slices in the air fryer. Do not stack. Cook in batches. Spray the tomato slices with cooking oil. Cook for 5 minutes.

6. Open the air fryer and flip the tomatoes. Cook for an additional 4 to 5 minutes, or until crisp.

7. Remove the cooked tomato slices from the air fryer, then repeat steps 5 and 6 for the remaining tomatoes.

Substitution tip: Standard bread crumbs can be used as a substitute for panko.

Ingredient tip: You can find unripe green tomatoes at Whole Foods or your local farmers' market.

Per serving: Calories: 167; Total fat: 3g; Saturated fat: 1g; Cholesterol: 82mg; Sodium: 96mg; Carbohydrates: 28g; Fiber: 3g; Protein: 7g

AREN'T YOU GLAD YOU DIDN'T DEEP-FRY?

Making your own fried green tomatoes gives you control over the oil used for the recipe. Olive oil, for instance, is loaded with monounsaturated fat, the good fat! Most restaurants fry their tomatoes in highly processed frying oil. Olive oil and the other oils mentioned in this book provide a healthier alternative.

Vegetable Fried Rice

FAMILY FAVORITE, VEGETARIAN

FRY: 375°F • PREP TIME: 5 MINUTES, PLUS 15 MINUTES TO
CHILL • COOK TIME: 20 MINUTES • SERVES 5

You won't turn to takeout once you make this recipe. This Asian-inspired air fryer veggie fried rice works wonderfully as a main dish or side. You will need a barrel accessory pan for this recipe.

2 (9-ounce) packages precooked, microwavable rice

2 teaspoons sesame oil, divided

1 medium green bell pepper, seeded and chopped

1 cup peas

2 medium carrots, diced (about 1 cup)

½ cup chopped onion

Salt

Pepper

1 tablespoon soy sauce

2 medium eggs, scrambled

1. Cook the rice in the microwave according to the package instructions and place in the refrigerator. The rice will need to cool for 15 to 20 minutes. You can also place it in the freezer until cold.

2. Add 1 teaspoon of sesame oil to the bottom of the barrel pan.

3. In a large bowl, combine the cold rice, green bell pepper, peas, carrots, and onion. Drizzle with the remaining 1 teaspoon of sesame oil and stir. Add salt and pepper to taste.

4. Transfer the mixture to the barrel pan. Cook for 15 minutes.

5. Remove the barrel pan. Drizzle the soy sauce all over and add the scrambled eggs. Stir to combine.

6. Serve warm.

Substitution tip: I use sesame oil in this recipe because it provides a distinctly Asian-style flavor. You can substitute canola, olive, or grapeseed oil, but you will lose a layer of flavor as those oils are neutral in taste.

Variation tip: Brown or white rice will work for this recipe. Both will have the same cook time if using precooked rice.

Per serving: Calories: 191; Total fat: 4g; Saturated fat: 1g; Cholesterol: 65mg; Sodium: 255mg; Carbohydrates: 32g; Fiber: 4g; Protein: 7g

Vegetarian Stuffed Peppers

FAST, VEGETARIAN

ROAST: 350° • PREP TIME: 15 MINUTES • COOK TIME: 15 MINUTES • SERVES 4

These veggie-stuffed peppers pair well with a side salad or steamed veggies. Use your favorite cooked rice—brown and white work equally well—and your go-to pasta sauce. I prefer to use organic precooked rice that can be prepared in the microwave. Trader Joe's has several options.

4 large red bell peppers

1½ cups cooked rice

¼ cup chopped onion

¼ cup sliced mushrooms

¾ cup marinara sauce

Salt

Pepper

¾ cup shredded mozzarella cheese

1. Boil a large pot of water over high heat.

2. Cut off the tops of the peppers. You can save the tops for decorative plating after you have cooked the peppers. Remove the seeds and hollow out the inside of the peppers.

3. Add the peppers to the boiling water for 5 minutes. Remove and allow them to cool for 3 to 4 minutes.

4. In a large bowl, combine the cooked rice, onion, mushrooms, and marinara sauce. Season with salt and pepper to taste.

5. Stuff the peppers with the rice mixture. Sprinkle the mozzarella cheese on top of the peppers.

6. Place the stuffed peppers in the air fryer. Cook for 10 minutes.

7. Cool before serving.

Prep tip: These can be prepared in advance. Wrap the stuffed peppers in foil and store in the refrigerator. You can pop them in the air fryer for a quick weeknight meal.

Per serving: Calories: 188; Total fat: 3g; Saturated fat: 1g; Cholesterol: 4mg; Sodium: 266mg; Carbohydrates: 36g; Fiber: 3g; Protein: 5g

Roasted Corn on the Cob

FAST, FAMILY FAVORITE, VEGETARIAN, GLUTEN-FREE

ROAST: 390°F • PREP TIME: 10 MINUTES • COOK TIME: 10 MINUTES • SERVES 4

When cooked in the air fryer, this Roasted Corn on the Cob tastes like it was grilled outdoors. And it's ready in minutes; there's no need to wait for the grill to get to temperature. Slather with butter and serve alongside your barbecue favorites.

4 ears corn, shucked and halved crosswise

1 tablespoon extra-virgin olive oil

Salt

Pepper

1. Place the corn in a large bowl. Coat with the olive oil and season with salt and pepper to taste.

2. Place the corn in the air fryer. Cook for 6 minutes.

3. Cool before serving.

Substitution tip: You can use 1 tablespoon melted butter instead of olive oil.

Per serving: Calories: 93; Total fat: 4g; Saturated fat: 1g; Cholesterol: 0mg; Sodium: 50mg; Carbohydrates: 14g; Fiber: 2g; Protein: 2g

Loaded Sweet Potatoes

FAMILY FAVORITE, VEGETARIAN, GLUTEN-FREE

BAKE: 390°F • PREP TIME: 5 MINUTES • COOK TIME: 40 MINUTES • SERVES 4

This recipe reminds me of the candied yams my family eats during the holidays. Baking sweet potatoes in the air fryer saves so much time compared to cooking in the oven or boiling: What normally takes more than an hour shrinks to a mere 40 minutes.

4 sweet potatoes

2 tablespoons butter

2 tablespoons honey

1 teaspoon cinnamon

½ teaspoon vanilla extract

1. Using a fork, poke three holes in the top of each sweet potato.

2. Place the sweet potatoes in the air fryer. Cook for 40 minutes.

3. Meanwhile, in a small, microwave-safe bowl, melt the butter and honey together in the microwave for 15 to 20 seconds.

4. Remove the bowl from the microwave. Add the cinnamon and vanilla extract to the butter and honey mixture, and stir.

5. Remove the cooked sweet potatoes from the air fryer and allow them to cool for 5 minutes.

6. Cut open each sweet potato. Drizzle the butter mixture over each, and serve.

Cooking tip: Poke the potatoes with a fork or knife to monitor doneness. The inside should be soft.

Per serving: Calories: 198; Total fat: 6g; Saturated fat: 4g; Cholesterol: 15mg; Sodium: 113mg; Carbohydrates: 35g; Fiber: 4g; Protein: 3g

Roasted Brown Butter Carrots

FAST, FAMILY FAVORITE, VEGETARIAN, GLUTEN-FREE

ROAST: 390°F • PREP TIME: 5 MINUTES • COOK TIME: 20 MINUTES • SERVES 4

This recipe elevates regular old carrots into something to savor. Brown butter has a nutty, toasted flavor that gives this vegetable a surprising richness. Cooked until tender in the air fryer, these roasted carrots pair beautifully with chicken and beef dishes.

1 tablespoon
  unsalted butter

6 carrots, cut into ½-inch
  pieces (about 3 cups)

Salt

Pepper

1. Place a saucepan over high heat. Add the butter. Allow the butter to melt for 2 to 3 minutes.

2. Stirring constantly to ensure it does not scorch, cook for 1 to 2 minutes, until it starts to turn brown. Brown bits will form on the bottom of the pan. Remove the pan from heat.

3. In a large bowl, combine the carrots with the brown butter. Season with salt and pepper to taste.

4. Transfer the carrots to the air fryer. Cook for 6 minutes.

5. Open the air fryer and shake the basket. Cook for an additional 6 minutes.

6. Cool before serving.

Per serving: Calories: 63; Total fat: 3g; Saturated fat: 2g; Cholesterol: 8mg; Sodium: 122mg; Carbohydrates: 9g; Fiber: 2g; Protein: 1g

Cilantro-Lime Fried Shrimp, page 88

CHAPTER 6

Fish and Seafood

Cilantro-Lime Fried Shrimp

FAMILY FAVORITE

FRY: 400°F • PREP TIME: 10 MINUTES, PLUS 30 MINUTES TO MARINATE • COOK TIME: 10 MINUTES • SERVES 4

The zesty, bold flavors in this recipe celebrate spring and summer. Marinating the shrimp makes up most of the prep time (you will need a sealable plastic bag for this step). Feel free to use fresh or thawed frozen shrimp for this recipe. These shrimp are excellent dipped in cocktail sauce.

1 pound raw shrimp, peeled and deveined with tails on or off (see Prep tip)

½ cup chopped fresh cilantro

Juice of 1 lime

1 egg

½ cup all-purpose flour

¾ cup bread crumbs

Salt

Pepper

Cooking oil

½ cup cocktail sauce (optional)

1. Place the shrimp in a plastic bag and add the cilantro and lime juice. Seal the bag. Shake to combine. Marinate in the refrigerator for 30 minutes.

2. In a small bowl, beat the egg. In another small bowl, place the flour. Place the bread crumbs in a third small bowl, and season with salt and pepper to taste.

3. Spray the air fryer basket with cooking oil.

4. Remove the shrimp from the plastic bag. Dip each in the flour, then the egg, and then the bread crumbs.

5. Place the shrimp in the air fryer. It is okay to stack them. Spray the shrimp with cooking oil. Cook for 4 minutes.

6. Open the air fryer and flip the shrimp. I recommend flipping individually instead of shaking to keep the breading intact. Cook for an additional 4 minutes, or until crisp.

7. Cool before serving. Serve with cocktail sauce if desired.

Substitution tip: You can reduce the amount of calories and fat in this recipe by substituting an egg white for the whole egg.

Prep tip: If using frozen shrimp, place the shrimp in a large bowl of cold water to thaw. Allow the shrimp to soak for 15 minutes.

Per serving: Calories: 254; Total fat: 4g; Saturated fat: 1g; Cholesterol: 221mg; Sodium: 334mg; Carbohydrates: 27g; Fiber: 1g; Protein: 29g

Salmon Croquettes

FAST, FAMILY FAVORITE

FRY: 400°F • PREP TIME: 5 MINUTES • COOK TIME: 15 MINUTES
MAKES 6 CROQUETTES (1 CROQUETTE = 1 SERVING)

Salmon croquettes are a classic recipe traditionally prepared in a cast iron skillet. The croquettes are usually fried in butter or oil, sometimes a combination of both! This lightened-up version does not compromise on taste. Serve the croquettes with tartar sauce, mayonnaise, or a squeeze of fresh lemon juice.

1 (14.75-ounce) can Alaskan pink salmon, drained and bones removed

1 egg, beaten

½ cup bread crumbs

2 scallions, diced

1 teaspoon garlic powder

Salt

Pepper

Cooking oil

1. In a large bowl, combine the salmon, beaten egg, bread crumbs, and scallions. Season with the garlic powder and salt and pepper to taste.

2. Form the mixture into 6 patties.

3. Place the croquettes in the air fryer. It is okay to stack them. Spray the croquettes with cooking oil. Cook for 7 minutes.

4. Open the air fryer and flip the patties. Cook for an additional 3 to 4 minutes, or until golden brown.

5. Serve.

Per serving: Calories: 142; Total fat: 6g; Saturated fat: 1g; Cholesterol: 58mg; Sodium: 135mg; Carbohydrates: 7g; Fiber: 1g; Protein: 16g

AREN'T YOU GLAD YOU DIDN'T DEEP-FRY?

Turning this home-style favorite into an air fryer recipe cuts the fat by more than half.

Beer-Battered Fish and Chips

FAMILY FAVORITE

FRY: 400°F • PREP TIME: 5 MINUTES • COOK TIME: 30 MINUTES • SERVES 4

When I visited London years ago, I made sure to order fish and chips pretty much everywhere I went. Beer-battered fish has a little more flavor. Malty beer will work best for this recipe—I like to use Pabst Blue Ribbon. Pair your crispy fried cod with Classic French Fries (page 44).

2 eggs

1 cup malty beer, such as Pabst Blue Ribbon

1 cup all-purpose flour

½ cup cornstarch

1 teaspoon garlic powder

Salt

Pepper

Cooking oil

4 (4-ounce) cod fillets

1. In a medium bowl, beat the eggs with the beer. In another medium bowl, combine the flour and cornstarch, and season with the garlic powder and salt and pepper to taste.

2. Spray the air fryer basket with cooking oil.

3. Dip each cod fillet in the flour and cornstarch mixture and then in the egg and beer mixture. Dip the cod in the flour and cornstarch a second time.

4. Place the cod in the air fryer. Do not stack. Cook in batches. Spray with cooking oil. Cook for 8 minutes.

5. Open the air fryer and flip the cod. Cook for an additional 7 minutes.

6. Remove the cooked cod from the air fryer, then repeat steps 4 and 5 for the remaining fillets.

7. Serve with Classic French Fries (page 44) or prepare air-fried frozen fries. Frozen fries will need to be cooked for 18 to 20 minutes at 400°F.

8. Cool before serving.

AREN'T YOU GLAD YOU DIDN'T DEEP-FRY?

Ordering one battered fish fillet with chips at a fast-food chain will cost you 26 grams of fat. This recipe has a fraction of that thanks to the air fryer.

Per serving: Calories: 325; Total fat: 4g; Saturated fat: 1g; Cholesterol: 137mg; Sodium: 144mg; Carbohydrates: 41g; Fiber: 1g; Protein: 26g

Firecracker Shrimp

FAST, FAMILY FAVORITE

FRY: 400°F • PREP TIME: 10 MINUTES • COOK TIME: 10 MINUTES • SERVES 4

Spicy foods are my favorite. The firecracker dipping sauce in this recipe does not disappoint. These shrimp are fried to perfection and then served alongside a spicy-sweet chili sauce.

For the shrimp

1 pound raw shrimp, peeled and deveined (see Prep tip, page 88)

Salt

Pepper

1 egg

½ cup all-purpose flour

¾ cup panko bread crumbs

Cooking oil

For the firecracker sauce

⅓ cup sour cream

2 tablespoons Sriracha

¼ cup sweet chili sauce

To make the shrimp

1. Season the shrimp with salt and pepper to taste.

2. In a small bowl, beat the egg.

3. In another small bowl, place the flour. In a third small bowl, add the panko bread crumbs.

4. Spray the air fryer basket with cooking oil.

5. Dip the shrimp in the flour, then the egg, and then the bread crumbs.

6. Place the shrimp in the air fryer basket. It is okay to stack them. Spray the shrimp with cooking oil. Cook for 4 minutes.

7. Open the air fryer and flip the shrimp. I recommend flipping individually instead of shaking to keep the breading intact.

8. Cook for an additional 4 minutes or until crisp.

To make the firecracker sauce

1. While the shrimp is cooking, make the firecracker sauce: In a small bowl, combine the sour cream, Sriracha, and sweet chili sauce. Mix well.

2. Serve with the shrimp.

Substitution tip: In place of sour cream, use nonfat plain Greek yogurt. This saves calories and fat while providing 5.5 grams additional protein.

Per serving: Calories: 266; Total fat: 6g; Saturated fat: 3g; Cholesterol: 229mg; Sodium: 393mg; Carbohydrates: 23g; Fiber: 1g; Protein: 27g

Crab Cakes

FAST, FAMILY FAVORITE

FRY: 375°F • PREP TIME: 5 MINUTES • COOK TIME: 10 MINUTES • SERVES 4

Crab cakes work well as both an appetizer and a main dish. In the air fryer, this satisfying recipe flavored with classic Old Bay Seasoning takes only 15 minutes to prepare! Serve as a side or on a bun with mayo and lettuce to create a crab cake sandwich.

8 ounces jumbo lump crabmeat

1 tablespoon Old Bay Seasoning

⅓ cup bread crumbs

¼ cup diced red bell pepper

¼ cup diced green bell pepper

1 egg

¼ cup mayonnaise

Juice of ½ lemon

1 teaspoon flour

Cooking oil

1. In a large bowl, combine the crabmeat, Old Bay Seasoning, bread crumbs, red bell pepper, green bell pepper, egg, mayo, and lemon juice. Mix gently to combine.

2. Form the mixture into 4 patties. Sprinkle ¼ teaspoon of flour on top of each patty.

3. Place the crab cakes in the air fryer. Spray them with cooking oil. Cook for 10 minutes.

4. Serve.

Ingredient tip: You can make your own crab seasoning using ¼ teaspoon of each of the following: celery salt, black pepper, red pepper flakes, and paprika.

Per serving: Calories: 176; Total fat: 8g; Saturated fat: 1g; Cholesterol: 101mg; Sodium: 826mg; Carbohydrates: 12g; Fiber: 1g; Protein: 15g

Coconut Shrimp

FAST, FAMILY FAVORITE

FRY: 400°F • PREP TIME: 10 MINUTES • COOK TIME: 10 MINUTES • SERVES 4

If you are really strapped for time, use this irresistible Coconut Shrimp recipe to get dinner on the table in little to no time. This family favorite pairs well with a side salad or rice and steamed veggies.

1 pound raw shrimp, peeled and deveined (see Prep tip, page 88)

1 egg

¼ cup all-purpose flour

⅓ cup shredded unsweetened coconut

¼ cup panko bread crumbs

Salt

Pepper

Cooking oil

1. Dry the shrimp with paper towels.
2. In a small bowl, beat the egg. In another small bowl, place the flour. In a third small bowl, combine the coconut and panko bread crumbs, and season with salt and pepper to taste. Mix well.
3. Spray the air fryer basket with cooking oil.
4. Dip the shrimp in the flour, then the egg, and then the coconut and bread crumb mixture.
5. Place the shrimp in the air fryer. It is okay to stack them. Cook for 4 minutes.
6. Open the air fryer and flip the shrimp. I recommend flipping individually instead of shaking, which keeps the breading intact. Cook for an additional 4 minutes or until crisp.
7. Cool before serving.

Per serving: Calories: 182; Total fat: 6g; Saturated fat: 3g; Cholesterol: 246mg; Sodium: 780mg; Carbohydrates: 8g; Fiber: 1g; Protein: 24g

Lemon-Pepper Tilapia with Garlic Aioli

FAST, FAMILY FAVORITE

BAKE: 400°F • PREP TIME: 5 MINUTES • COOK TIME: 15 MINUTES • SERVES 4

Impress picky eaters with this restaurant-quality dish. Fish baked in the air fryer comes out very moist and tender. The garlic aioli is prepared with fresh garlic and lemon. It is a sauce that pairs beautifully with chicken dishes and works for vegetable dipping as well.

For the tilapia

4 tilapia fillets (see Prep tip)

1 tablespoon extra-virgin olive oil

1 teaspoon paprika

1 teaspoon garlic powder

1 teaspoon dried basil

Lemon-pepper seasoning (such as McCormick Perfect Pinch Lemon & Pepper Seasoning)

For the garlic aioli

2 garlic cloves, minced

1 tablespoon mayonnaise

1 teaspoon extra-virgin olive oil

Juice of ½ lemon

Salt

Pepper

To make the tilapia

1. Coat the fish with the olive oil. Season with the paprika, garlic powder, dried basil, and lemon-pepper seasoning.

2. Place the fish in the air fryer. It is okay to stack the fish. Cook for 8 minutes.

3. Open the air fryer and flip the fish. Cook for an additional 7 minutes.

To make the garlic aioli

1. In a small bowl, combine the garlic, mayonnaise, olive oil, lemon juice, and salt and pepper to taste. Whisk well to combine.

2. Serve alongside the fish.

Variation tip: This recipe can be made gluten-free by using gluten-free mayonnaise; be sure to check the label.

Ingredient tip: You can make your own lemon-pepper seasoning using the juice of ½ lemon and pepper to taste.

Prep tip: If using frozen tilapia, the best way to thaw it is in a covered bowl in the refrigerator, overnight. You can also place the fish in a sealed plastic bag and submerge the bag in cold water for 15 minutes or until thawed.

Per serving: Calories: 155; Total fat: 7g; Saturated fat: 1g; Cholesterol: 56mg; Sodium: 107mg; Carbohydrates: 2g; Fiber: 0g; Protein: 21g

Blackened Shrimp

FAST, FAMILY FAVORITE, GLUTEN-FREE

GRILL: 400°F • PREP TIME: 5 MINUTES • COOK TIME: 10 MINUTES • SERVES 4

This breading-free, low-carb Blackened Shrimp packs a lot of flavor into a small package. I like to serve this dish as a main along with Crunchy Green Beans (page 74) for a clean-eating meal. You will need a sealable plastic bag to marinate the shrimp for this recipe. Use a grill pan or the air fryer basket to cook it.

1 pound raw shrimp, peeled and deveined (see Prep tip, page 88)

1 teaspoon paprika

½ teaspoon dried oregano

½ teaspoon cayenne pepper

Juice of ½ lemon

Salt

Pepper

Cooking oil

1. Place the shrimp in a sealable plastic bag and add the paprika, oregano, cayenne pepper, lemon juice, and salt and pepper to taste. Seal the bag and shake well to combine.

2. Spray a grill pan or the air fryer basket with cooking oil.

3. Place the shrimp in the air fryer. It is okay to stack the shrimp. Cook for 4 minutes.

4. Open the air fryer and shake the basket. Cook for an additional 3 to 4 minutes, or until the shrimp has blackened.

5. Cool before serving.

Variation tip: This shrimp is delicious over a green salad with avocado. Dress it with a simple cilantro-lime vinaigrette made from chopped fresh cilantro, lime juice, and olive oil.

Per serving: Calories: 101; Total fat: 2g; Saturated fat: 2g; Cholesterol: 168mg; Sodium: 759mg; Carbohydrates: 0g; Fiber: 0g; Protein: 21g

Fried Catfish Nuggets

FAMILY FAVORITE

FRY: 400°F • PREP TIME: 5 MINUTES • COOK TIME: 40 MINUTES • SERVES 4

I love this recipe because it uses only three ingredients. My family grew up using the Louisiana Fish Fry brand of seasoned breading mix. This brand crisps the fish perfectly! You can find it in the fresh seafood area of the grocery store or online. There certainly are other brands to try. However, you can also make your own. For a great result, simply mix together ½ cup cornmeal, ½ teaspoon garlic powder, ½ teaspoon onion powder, ½ teaspoon cayenne pepper, and salt and pepper to taste. You will need a sealable plastic bag for this recipe.

1 pound catfish fillets, cut into 1-inch chunks

½ cup seasoned fish fry breading mix (such as Louisiana Fish Fry)

Cooking oil

AREN'T YOU GLAD YOU DIDN'T DEEP-FRY?

The air fryer saves 5 grams of fat per serving compared to restaurant catfish nuggets.

1. Rinse and thoroughly dry the catfish. Pour the seasoned fish fry breading mix into a sealable plastic bag and add the catfish. (You may need to use two bags depending on the size of your nuggets.) Seal the bag and shake to evenly coat the fish with breading.

2. Spray the air fryer basket with cooking oil.

3. Transfer the catfish nuggets to the air fryer. Do not overcrowd the basket. You may need to cook the nuggets in two batches. Spray the nuggets with cooking oil. Cook for 10 minutes.

4. Open the air fryer and shake the basket. Cook for an additional 8 to 10 minutes, or until the fish is crisp.

5. If necessary, remove the cooked catfish nuggets from the air fryer, then repeat steps 3 and 4 for the remaining fish.

6. Cool before serving.

Ingredient tip: You may be able to purchase catfish nuggets at the fish counter of your grocery store. It's worth asking!

Cooking tip: Open the air fryer and check in on the fish a few times throughout the cooking process. When the fish has turned golden brown on both sides, it has finished cooking.

Per serving: Calories: 183; Total fat: 9g; Saturated fat: 2g; Cholesterol: 56mg; Sodium: 199mg; Carbohydrates: 5g; Fiber: 0g; Protein: 19g

Cornmeal Shrimp Po'Boy

FAST, FAMILY FAVORITE

FRY: 400°F • PREP TIME: 10 MINUTES • COOK TIME: 10 MINUTES • SERVES 4

You cannot go wrong with classic cornmeal-breaded shrimp, and here we present it New Orleans–style. The traditional Southern po'boy is served on a French baguette, but feel free to use any kind of roll you have on hand. Crispy shrimp and a kick of remoulade highlight the dish.

For the shrimp

1 pound shrimp, peeled and deveined (see Prep tip, page 88)

1 egg

½ cup flour

¾ cup cornmeal

Salt

Pepper

Cooking oil

For the remoulade

½ cup mayonnaise

1 teaspoon mustard (I use Dijon)

1 teaspoon Worcestershire

1 teaspoon minced garlic

Juice of ½ lemon

1 teaspoon Sriracha

½ teaspoon Creole seasoning (I use Tony Chachere's brand)

For the po'boys

4 rolls

2 cups shredded lettuce

8 slices tomato

To make the shrimp

1. Dry the shrimp with paper towels.

2. In a small bowl, beat the egg. In another small bowl, place the flour. Place the cornmeal in a third small bowl, and season with salt and pepper to taste.

3. Spray the air fryer basket with cooking oil.

4. Dip the shrimp in the flour, then the egg, and then the cornmeal.

5. Place the shrimp in the air fryer. Cook for 4 minutes. Open the basket and flip the shrimp. Cook for an additional 4 minutes, or until crisp.

To make the remoulade

While the shrimp is cooking, in a small bowl, combine the mayonnaise, mustard, Worcestershire, garlic, lemon juice, Sriracha, and Creole seasoning. Mix well.

To make the po'boys

1. Split the rolls and spread them with the remoulade.

2. Let the shrimp cool slightly before assembling the po'boys.

3. Fill each roll with a quarter of the shrimp, ½ cup of shredded lettuce, and 2 slices of tomato. Serve.

Per serving: Calories: 483; Total fat: 15g; Saturated fat: 2g; Cholesterol: 229mg; Sodium: 690mg; Carbohydrates: 58g; Fiber: 6g; Protein: 32g

Spicy Coconut Chicken Wings, page 107

CHAPTER 7

Poultry

Italian Chicken Parmesan

FAST, FAMILY FAVORITE

FRY: 370°F • PREP TIME: 10 MINUTES • COOK TIME: 20 MINUTES • SERVES 4

Goodbye, deep-fried chicken; hello, crunchy chicken cutlets using the air fryer. This recipe may become your go-to dinner on weeknights when time is scarce and you have an entire family to feed. The combination of melted mozzarella cheese and crunchy breading in this recipe is irresistible.

2 (4-ounce) boneless, skinless chicken breasts

1 cup Italian bread crumbs

½ cup grated Parmesan cheese

2 teaspoons Italian seasoning

Salt

Pepper

2 egg whites

Cooking oil

¾ cup marinara sauce

½ cup shredded mozzarella cheese

1. With your knife blade parallel to the cutting board, slice the chicken breasts in half horizontally to create 4 thin cutlets.

2. On a solid surface, pound the cutlets to flatten them. You can use your hands, a rolling pin, a kitchen mallet, or a meat hammer.

3. In a bowl large enough to dip a chicken cutlet, combine the bread crumbs, Parmesan cheese, Italian seasoning, and salt and pepper to taste. Stir to combine.

4. Pour the egg whites into another bowl large enough to dip the chicken.

5. Spray the air fryer basket with cooking oil.

6. Dip each cutlet in the egg whites and then the bread crumb mixture.

7. Place 2 chicken cutlets in the air fryer basket. Spray the top of the chicken with cooking oil. Cook for 7 minutes.

8. Remove the cooked cutlets from the air fryer, then repeat step 7 with the remaining 2 cutlets.

9. Open the air fryer. Top the chicken cutlets with the marinara sauce and shredded mozzarella. If the chicken cutlets will fit in your air fryer without stacking, you can prepare all 4 at once. Otherwise, do this 2 cutlets at a time. Cook for an additional 3 minutes, or until the cheese has melted.

10. Cool before serving.

Air fryer cooking tip: Preparing this dish in batches yields the best results. The cook time noted above (20 minutes) is for cooking the chicken cutlets in two batches.

Per serving: Calories: 257; Total fat: 8g; Saturated fat: 3g; Cholesterol: 46mg; Sodium: 593mg; Carbohydrates: 23g; Fiber: 1g; Protein: 24g

Chicken Nuggets

FAST, FAMILY FAVORITE

FRY: 400°F • PREP TIME: 10 MINUTES • COOK TIME: 20 MINUTES • SERVES 4

Deep-fried chicken nuggets are loaded with fat, especially the nuggets you pick up in a drive-through. The air fryer provides a healthier option, but these are still the breaded and crisp nuggets children (and adults!) love. Serve with ketchup, ranch dressing, honey mustard, and a side of Classic French Fries (page 44).

1 pound boneless, skinless chicken breasts

Chicken seasoning or rub

Salt

Pepper

2 eggs

6 tablespoons bread crumbs

2 tablespoons panko bread crumbs

Cooking oil

1. Cut the chicken breasts into 1-inch pieces.
2. In a large bowl, combine the chicken pieces with chicken seasoning, salt, and pepper to taste.
3. In a small bowl, beat the eggs. In another bowl, combine the bread crumbs and panko.
4. Dip the chicken pieces in the eggs and then the bread crumbs.
5. Place the nuggets in the air fryer. Do not overcrowd the basket. Cook in batches. Spray the nuggets with cooking oil. Cook for 4 minutes.
6. Open the air fryer and shake the basket. Cook for an additional 4 minutes.
7. Remove the cooked nuggets from the air fryer, then repeat steps 5 and 6 for the remaining chicken nuggets.
8. Cool before serving.

Substitution tip: Don't worry if panko isn't one of your pantry staples. Additional regular bread crumbs can be used in its place.

Per serving: Calories: 206; Total fat: 5g; Saturated fat: 1g; Cholesterol: 147mg; Sodium: 267mg; Carbohydrates: 10g; Fiber: 1g; Protein: 31g

Fajita Stuffed Chicken Roll-Ups

FAMILY FAVORITE, GLUTEN-FREE

BAKE: 400°F • PREP TIME: 10 MINUTES • COOK TIME: 25 MINUTES • SERVES 4

This low-carb recipe loses the tortilla but retains the punchy flavor of a traditional fajita. Chicken breasts are stuffed with sliced peppers and onions, rolled up, and baked to perfection. You will need toothpicks for this recipe to secure your fajita rolls while air frying.

2 (4-ounce) boneless, skinless chicken breasts

Juice of ½ lime

2 tablespoons taco or fajita seasoning

½ red bell pepper, cut into strips

½ green bell pepper, cut into strips

¼ onion, sliced

Cooking oil

1. With your knife blade parallel to the cutting board, slice the chicken breasts in half horizontally to create 4 thin cutlets.

2. Drizzle the lime juice over the chicken cutlets, then season with the taco or fajita seasoning.

3. Place equal amounts of the red bell pepper strips, green bell pepper strips, and onion slices onto each of the chicken cutlets.

4. Roll up each cutlet and secure with toothpicks. The chicken will look like a cylinder.

5. Place 4 chicken roll-ups in the air fryer. Do not overcrowd the basket. Spray the chicken with cooking oil. Cook for 12 minutes.

6. Cool before serving.

Ingredient tip: Check the label to make sure your taco seasoning is gluten-free. Or make your own by combining 1 teaspoon chili powder, 1 teaspoon cumin, ¼ teaspoon onion powder, ¼ teaspoon dried oregano, and ¼ teaspoon paprika.

Per serving: Calories: 88; Total fat: 2g; Saturated fat: 0g; Cholesterol: 32mg; Sodium: 302mg; Carbohydrates: 6g; Fiber: 0g; Protein: 14g

Buffalo Chicken Wings

FAST, FAMILY FAVORITE, GLUTEN-FREE

FRY: 400°F • PREP TIME: 10 MINUTES • COOK TIME: 20 MINUTES • SERVES 6

Craving restaurant-style Buffalo wings but not the heartburn that often follows? The air fryer delivers a lighter, healthier Buffalo wing you can enjoy in the comfort of your own home. Whip up a batch for a snack or serve them for game night with celery sticks and blue cheese dressing.

16 chicken drumettes (party wings)

1 teaspoon garlic powder

Chicken seasoning or rub

Pepper

Cooking oil

¼ cup Frank's RedHot Buffalo Wings Sauce

1. Season the drumettes with the garlic powder and chicken seasoning and pepper to taste.

2. Place the chicken in the air fryer. It is okay to stack the drumettes on top of each other. Spray them with cooking oil. Cook for 5 minutes.

3. Remove the basket and shake it to ensure all of the pieces will cook fully. Cook for an additional 5 minutes.

4. Open the air fryer and transfer the drumettes to a large bowl. Toss the drumettes with the Buffalo wing sauce, ensuring each is covered.

5. Return the drumettes to the air fryer. Cook for 7 minutes.

6. Cool before serving.

Substitution tip: To make your own Buffalo sauce, combine 1 part melted butter to 2 parts Frank's RedHot Original. So, to make ¼ cup of sauce, combine 1½ tablespoons melted butter to 3 tablespoons Frank's RedHot.

Ingredient tip: Check the label to make sure your chicken seasoning is gluten-free.

Cooking tip: Use your judgment and preference to determine how long the chicken should cook. If you prefer really crispy chicken, you may need to allow your wings to cook longer than the time allotted above. Check in on the chicken at 5 minutes to ensure it has fully cooked on the inside.

Per serving: Calories: 189; Total fat: 8g; Saturated fat: 2g; Cholesterol: 107mg; Sodium: 429mg; Carbohydrates: 0g; Fiber: 0g; Protein: 29g

Buttermilk Country-Fried Chicken Wings

FAST, FAMILY FAVORITE

FRY: 400°F • PREP TIME: 10 MINUTES • COOK TIME: 20 MINUTES • SERVES 4

This recipe is dripping with the home-style fried chicken flavor I grew up with. Need an appetizer that is going to win over your guests? You can't go wrong with these chicken wings; they are great for gatherings, sporting events, and watch parties. You will need 2 sealable plastic bags for this recipe.

16 chicken drumettes
  (party wings)

1 teaspoon garlic powder

Chicken seasoning or rub

Pepper

½ cup all-purpose flour

¼ cup low-fat buttermilk

Cooking oil

1. Place the chicken in a sealable plastic bag. Add the garlic powder, then add chicken seasoning or rub and pepper to taste. Seal the bag. Shake the bag thoroughly to combine the seasonings and coat the chicken.

2. Pour the flour into a second sealable plastic bag.

3. Pour the buttermilk into a bowl large enough to dunk the chicken. One at a time, dunk the drumettes in the buttermilk, then place them in the bag of flour. Seal and shake to thoroughly coat the chicken.

4. Spray the air fryer basket with cooking oil.

5. Using tongs, transfer the chicken from the bag to the air fryer basket. It is okay to stack the drumettes on top of each other. Spray the chicken with cooking oil, being sure to cover the bottom layer. Cook for 5 minutes.

6. Remove the basket and shake it to ensure all of the chicken pieces will cook fully.

7. Return the basket to the air fryer and continue to cook the chicken. Repeat shaking every 5 minutes until 20 minutes has passed.

8. Cool before serving.

Variation tip: If you are looking for a dairy-free alternative, you can substitute egg whites for the buttermilk.

Ingredient tip: If you don't have buttermilk on hand, you can make your own. Simply add 1 teaspoon vinegar, lemon juice, or lime juice to ¼ cup low-fat milk. Stir, then let it sit for 5 minutes, or until the milk begins to curdle.

Per serving: Calories: 347; Total fat: 12g; Saturated fat: 3g; Cholesterol: 161mg; Sodium: 210mg; Carbohydrates: 13g; Fiber: 1g; Protein: 46g

Lemon-Pepper Chicken Wings

FAST, FAMILY FAVORITE

FRY: 400°F • PREP TIME: 10 MINUTES • COOK TIME: 20 MINUTE • SERVES 4

Lemon-Pepper Chicken Wings burst with zest and flavor. Freshly squeezed lemon juice is drizzled over the wings, seasoned with spices and buttermilk breading. The wings are air-fried and served crisp. You will need a sealable plastic bag for this recipe.

8 whole chicken wings
Juice of ½ lemon
½ teaspoon garlic powder
1 teaspoon onion powder
Salt
Pepper
¼ cup low-fat buttermilk
½ cup all-purpose flour
Cooking oil

AREN'T YOU GLAD YOU DIDN'T DEEP-FRY?

Air-frying your chicken wings saves 21 grams of fat per serving compared to deep-fried restaurant wings.

1. Place the wings in a sealable plastic bag. Drizzle the wings with the lemon juice. Season the wings with the garlic powder, onion powder, and salt and pepper to taste.

2. Seal the bag. Shake thoroughly to combine the seasonings and coat the wings.

3. Pour the buttermilk and the flour into separate bowls large enough to dip the wings.

4. Spray the air fryer basket with cooking oil.

5. One at a time, dip the wings in the buttermilk and then the flour.

6. Place the wings in the air fryer basket. It is okay to stack them on top of each other. Spray the wings with cooking oil, being sure to spray the bottom layer. Cook for 5 minutes.

7. Remove the basket and shake it to ensure all of the pieces will cook fully.

8. Return the basket to the air fryer and continue to cook the chicken. Repeat shaking every 5 minutes until a total of 20 minutes has passed.

9. Cool before serving.

Per serving: Calories: 347; Total fat: 12g; Saturated fat: 3g; Cholesterol: 161mg; Sodium: 246mg; Carbohydrates: 13g; Fiber: 1g; Protein: 46g

Spicy Coconut Chicken Wings

FAMILY FAVORITE

FRY: 400°F • PREP TIME: 10 MINUTES, PLUS 30 MINUTES TO
MARINATE • COOK TIME: 20 MINUTES • SERVES 4

Pair these spicy and sweet chicken wings with mango salsa and coconut rice for a picture of paradise. You will need a sealable plastic bag for this recipe.

For the coconut chicken

16 chicken drumettes
  (party wings)

¼ cup full-fat coconut milk

1 tablespoon Sriracha

1 teaspoon onion powder

1 teaspoon garlic powder

Salt

Pepper

⅓ cup shredded
  unsweetened coconut

½ cup all-purpose flour

Cooking oil

For the mango salsa

1 cup mango sliced into
  ½ inch chunks

¼ cup cilantro, chopped

½ cup red onion, chopped

2 garlic cloves, minced

Juice of ½ lime

To make the coconut chicken

1. Place the drumettes in a sealable plastic bag.
2. In a small bowl, combine the coconut milk and Sriracha. Whisk until fully combined.
3. Drizzle the drumettes with the spicy coconut milk mixture. Season the drumettes with the onion powder, garlic powder, and salt and pepper to taste.
4. Seal the bag. Shake it thoroughly to combine the seasonings and coat the chicken. Marinate for at least 30 minutes, preferably overnight, in the refrigerator.
5. When the drumettes are almost done marinating, combine the shredded coconut and flour in a large bowl. Stir.
6. Spray the air fryer basket with cooking oil.
7. Dip the drumettes in the coconut and flour mixture. Place them in the air fryer (it is okay to stack). Spray them with cooking oil. Cook for 5 minutes.
8. Remove the basket and shake it to ensure all of the pieces will cook fully.
9. Return the basket to the air fryer and continue to cook the chicken. Repeat shaking every 5 minutes until a total of 20 minutes has passed.
10. Cool before serving.

To make the mango salsa

While the chicken cooks, combine the mango, cilantro, red onion, garlic, and lime juice in a small bowl. Mix well until fully combined.

Per serving: Calories: 375; Total fat: 15g; Saturated fat: 6g; Cholesterol: 160mg; Sodium: 257mg; Carbohydrates: 14g; Fiber: 1g; Protein: 46g

Sweet-and-Sour Chicken

FAST, FAMILY FAVORITE

FRY: 360°F • PREP TIME: 15 MINUTES • COOK TIME: 15 MINUTES • SERVES 4

You no longer have to resort to takeout when a Chinese food craving hits! This chicken is fried until crispy and then drizzled in sweet-and-sour sauce. (Sweet-and-sour sauce can be found in the grocery store near the soy sauce.) Serve with Vegetable Fried Rice (page 81) and/or Crunchy Pork Egg Rolls (page 54) for a complete Asian-style feast.

1 cup cornstarch

Chicken seasoning or rub

Salt

Pepper

2 eggs

Cooking oil

2 (4-ounce) boneless, skinless chicken breasts, cut into 1-inch pieces

1½ cups sweet-and-sour sauce

1. In a large bowl, combine the cornstarch with chicken seasoning and salt and pepper to taste. Mix well.

2. In another bowl, beat the eggs.

3. Spray the air fryer basket with cooking oil.

4. Using a large spoon, dip the chicken in the cornstarch mixture, then the eggs, and then the cornstarch again.

5. Place the chicken in the air fryer basket. It is okay to stack the chicken pieces. Spray them with cooking oil. Cook for 8 minutes.

6. Open the air fryer and shake the basket. Cook the chicken for an additional 7 to 8 minutes, until it is golden brown and crisp.

7. Transfer the chicken to a serving dish. Drizzle the sweet-and-sour sauce over the chicken. Serve.

Substitution tip: To further reduce the fat and calories in this dish, substitute egg whites for the whole eggs, and reduce the amount of sweet-and-sour sauce to ½ cup.

Per serving: Calories: 325; Total fat: 3g; Saturated fat: 1g; Cholesterol: 114mg; Sodium: 427mg; Carbohydrates: 57g; Fiber: 1g; Protein: 16g

Honey Dijon Mustard Garlic Chicken

FAMILY FAVORITE

BAKE: 400°F • PREP TIME: 5 MINUTES • COOK TIME: 30 MINUTES • SERVES 4

Honey and Dijon mustard are a classic pairing that mixes sweet and tangy flavors. If you don't have Dijon mustard on hand, you can still make this with yellow mustard, but you'll end up with a milder-tasting dish. With the ease of creation in the air fryer, I often turn to this recipe for a quick weeknight dinner.

8 bone-in or boneless, skinless chicken thighs

Chicken seasoning or rub

Salt

Pepper

2 garlic cloves, minced

½ cup honey

¼ cup Dijon mustard

1. Season the thighs with chicken seasoning, salt, and pepper to taste.
2. Place 4 chicken thighs in the air fryer. Do not stack. You should not have to spray cooking oil, as the thighs will produce oil as they cook. Cook for 7 minutes.
3. Open the air fryer and flip the chicken. Cook for an additional 8 minutes.
4. Remove the cooked chicken, then repeat steps 2 and 3 for the remaining 4 chicken thighs.
5. While the chicken cooks, heat the garlic, honey, and Dijon mustard in a saucepan over medium-high heat. Stir to combine. Cook for 3 to 4 minutes, until the sauce thickens.
6. Transfer the chicken to a serving dish. Drizzle the chicken with the honey-Dijon sauce. Serve.

Ingredient tip: Bone-in or boneless thighs will work for this recipe. Bone-in thighs are juicier.

Per serving: Calories: 382; Total fat: 18g; Saturated fat: 5g; Cholesterol: 95mg; Sodium: 327mg; Carbohydrates: 36g; Fiber: 1g; Protein: 21g

Chicken and Veggie Kabobs

FAMILY FAVORITE, GLUTEN-FREE

GRILL: 360°F • PREP TIME: 10 MINUTES • COOK TIME: 45 MINUTES • SERVES 5

In the summer months, my mind turns to entertaining outdoors and then naturally to kabobs. When you don't have an outdoor grill, your air fryer comes to the rescue. Get creative with what you have on hand: cherry tomatoes, zucchini, and pineapple chunks all make great additions. You will need 10 to 15 wooden skewers for this recipe.

4 (4-ounce) boneless, skinless chicken breasts, cut into 1-inch cubes

Chicken seasoning or rub

Salt

Pepper

1 green bell pepper, seeded and cut into 1-inch pieces

1 red bell pepper, seeded and cut into 1-inch pieces

½ red onion, cut into 1-inch pieces

Cooking oil

1. Season the chicken with chicken seasoning, salt, and pepper to taste.
2. Thread wooden skewers with the cubed chicken, green bell pepper, red bell pepper, and onion.
3. Spray the air fryer basket with cooking oil.
4. Place the kabobs in the air fryer 4 or 5 at a time, depending on what fits in your unit. Do not overcrowd. You can use an accessory grill pan or rack, or place the kabobs directly into the air fryer basket. Spray the kabobs with cooking oil. Cook for 8 minutes.
5. Open the air fryer and flip the kabobs. Cook for an additional 7 minutes.
6. Remove the cooked kabobs from the air fryer, then repeat steps 4 and 5 for the remaining kabobs.
7. Cool before serving.

Ingredient tip: Check the label to make sure your chicken seasoning is gluten-free.

Prep tip: Soak the wooden skewers in water for 15 minutes prior to use. This will prevent the skewers from burning.

Per serving: Calories: 114; Total fat: 1g; Saturated fat: 0g; Cholesterol: 52mg; Sodium: 112mg; Carbohydrates: 4g; Fiber: 1g; Protein: 21g

Crispy Chicken and Pickles Sandwich

FAMILY FAVORITE

FRY: 370°F • PREP TIME: 10 MINUTES, PLUS 30 MINUTES TO MARINATE • COOK TIME: 25 MINUTES • SERVES 4

Make crispy chicken sandwiches at home that rival Chick-fil-A! These sandwiches are marinated in pickle juice to add a hint of pickle to the breading. Serve on buns with Classic French Fries (page 44) or air-fried frozen waffle fries on the side.

2 (4-ounce) boneless, skinless chicken breasts

1 cup dill pickle juice

1 cup milk, divided

Cooking oil

1 egg

½ cup all-purpose flour

Salt

Pepper

4 buns

Pickles

1. With your knife blade parallel to the cutting board, slice the chicken breasts in half horizontally to create 4 thin cutlets.

2. Place the chicken in a large bowl. Add the pickle juice and ½ cup of milk, and toss to coat.

3. Allow the chicken to marinate in the refrigerator for at least 30 minutes.

4. Spray the air fryer pan with cooking oil.

5. In a bowl large enough to dip a chicken cutlet, beat the egg and add the remaining ½ cup of milk. Stir to combine. In another bowl, place the flour and season with salt and pepper.

6. When done marinating, dip each chicken cutlet in the egg and milk mixture and then the flour.

7. Place 2 chicken cutlets in the air fryer. Spray them with cooking oil. Cook for 6 minutes.

8. Open the air fryer and flip the chicken. Cook for an additional 6 minutes.

9. Remove the cooked chicken from the air fryer, then repeat steps 7 and 8 for the remaining 2 chicken cutlets.

10. Serve on buns with pickles.

Ingredient tip: Did you know you can actually buy dill pickle juice online? Companies sell it by the gallon on Amazon! Of course, you can also just drain the juice from your dill pickle jar.

Per serving: Calories: 282; Total fat: 5g; Saturated fat: 1g; Cholesterol: 78mg; Sodium: 1116mg; Carbohydrates: 38g; Fiber: 2g; Protein: 21g

Crunchy Chicken and Ranch Wraps

FAST, FAMILY FAVORITE

FRY: 370°F • PREP TIME: 10 MINUTES • COOK TIME: 25 MINUTES • SERVES 4

My mouth waters just thinking about this dish. Chicken is coated with ranch seasoning, then breaded and air-fried. In 30 minutes, you can have a satisfying, crunchy chicken "wrap" on the table. I like to serve it open-faced, but if you prefer the tortilla wrapped, go for it!

2 (4-ounce) boneless, skinless breasts

½ (1-ounce) packet Hidden Valley Ranch seasoning mix

Chicken seasoning or rub

1 cup all-purpose flour

1 egg

½ cup bread crumbs

Cooking oil

4 medium (8-inch) flour tortillas

1½ cups shredded lettuce

3 tablespoons ranch dressing

1. With your knife blade parallel to the cutting board, slice the chicken breasts in half horizontally to create 4 thin cutlets.
2. Season the chicken cutlets with the ranch seasoning and chicken seasoning to taste.
3. In a bowl large enough to dip a chicken cutlet, beat the egg. In another bowl, place the flour. Put the bread crumbs in a third bowl.
4. Spray the air fryer basket with cooking oil.
5. Dip each chicken cutlet in the flour, then the egg, and then the bread crumbs.
6. Place the chicken in the air fryer. Do not stack. Cook in batches. Spray the chicken with cooking oil. Cook for 7 minutes.
7. Open the air fryer and flip the chicken. Cook for an additional 3 to 4 minutes, until crisp.
8. Remove the cooked chicken from the air fryer and allow to cool for 2 to 3 minutes.
9. Repeat steps 6 through 8 for the remaining chicken.
10. Cut the chicken into strips. Divide the chicken strips, shredded lettuce, and ranch dressing evenly among the tortillas and serve.

AREN'T YOU GLAD YOU DIDN'T DEEP-FRY?

You will save 8 grams of fat per serving by preparing your own air-fried chicken wrap instead of ordering from a drive-through restaurant.

Ingredient tip: You can find ranch seasoning packets in the condiments aisle of the grocery store, near the salad dressing.

Per serving: Calories: 303; Total fat: 5g; Saturated fat: 1g; Cholesterol: 58mg; Sodium: 398mg; Carbohydrates: 46g; Fiber: 3g; Protein: 18g

Bruschetta-Stuffed Chicken

FAST, FAMILY FAVORITE, GLUTEN-FREE

BAKE: 370°F • PREP TIME: 10 MINUTES • COOK TIME: 20 MINUTES • SERVES 4

I enjoy dining out at Italian restaurants primarily for the bread. Simple bruschetta usually consists of grilled bread with garlic, olive oil, and tomatoes. Another common version includes balsamic vinegar, fresh basil, and mozzarella. This low-carb recipe replaces the bread with chicken for a protein-rich variation.

For the bruschetta stuffing

2 tablespoons extra-virgin olive oil

3 tablespoons balsamic vinegar

3 garlic cloves, minced

1 tomato, diced

1 teaspoon Italian seasoning

2 tablespoons chopped fresh basil

For the chicken

4 (4-ounce) boneless, skinless chicken breasts

1 teaspoon Italian seasoning

Chicken seasoning or rub

Cooking oil

To make the bruschetta stuffing

In a medium bowl, combine the olive oil, balsamic vinegar, garlic, tomato, Italian seasoning, and basil. Set aside.

To make the chicken

1. Cut 4 or 5 slits into each chicken breast, without cutting all the way through.

2. Season the chicken with the Italian seasoning and chicken seasoning to taste.

3. Spray the air fryer basket with cooking oil.

4. Place the chicken (with the slits facing up) in the air fryer. Do not stack. Cook in batches. Spray the chicken with cooking oil. Cook for 7 minutes.

5. Open the air fryer and stuff the bruschetta mixture into the slits of the chicken. Cook for an additional 3 minutes.

6. Remove the cooked chicken from the air fryer, then repeat steps 4 and 5 for the remaining chicken breasts.

7. Cool before serving.

Ingredient tip: Check the labels to make sure your Italian seasoning and chicken seasoning are gluten-free.

Per serving: Calories: 197; Total fat: 9g; Saturated fat: 1g; Cholesterol: 67mg; Sodium: 101mg; Carbohydrates: 2g; Fiber: 0g; Protein: 26g

Honey BBQ Chicken Drumsticks

FAMILY FAVORITE

FRY: 390°F • PREP TIME: 5 MINUTES • COOK TIME: 40 MINUTES • SERVES 5

These sweet and savory drumsticks are a big hit with little ones. With the air fryer, you can provide a healthy, protein-packed snack for your kids without worrying about fat. The honey pairs well with all sauce varieties: sweet, spicy, or vinegar based.

10 chicken drumsticks

Chicken seasoning or rub

Salt

Pepper

Cooking oil

¼ cup honey

1 cup barbecue sauce

1. Season the drumsticks with chicken seasoning, salt, and pepper to taste.
2. Spray the air fryer basket with cooking oil.
3. Place the drumsticks in the air fryer. Do not stack. Cook in batches. Spray the chicken with cooking oil. Cook for 10 minutes.
4. Open the air fryer and flip the drumsticks. Cook for an additional 8 minutes.
5. Remove the cooked drumsticks from the air fryer, then repeat steps 3 and 4 for the remaining drumsticks.
6. In a small bowl, combine the honey and barbecue sauce. Drizzle the sauce over the drumsticks and serve.

Variation tip: Make this recipe gluten-free by using gluten-free barbecue sauce. Be sure to check the label.

Cooking tip: Check in on the chicken throughout the cooking process to check for doneness. The chicken has finished cooking when the skin is crisp. You can test the meat using a fork. The fork should go in with ease and the juices should run clear.

Per serving: Calories: 296; Total fat: 12g; Saturated fat: 3g; Cholesterol: 76mg; Sodium: 682mg; Carbohydrates: 32g; Fiber: 0g; Protein: 17g

Spinach and Cream Cheese Stuffed Chicken

FAST, FAMILY FAVORITE, GLUTEN-FREE

BAKE: 370°F • PREP TIME: 10 MINUTES • COOK TIME: 20 MINUTES • SERVES 4

This dish is far from boring! A sophisticated meal you can pull together in 30 minutes, it highlights Mediterranean flavors. Serve with a simple tomato and cucumber salad dressed with olive oil, salt, and pepper.

For the filling

⅓ cup cream cheese

1 cup chopped
  fresh spinach

For the chicken

4 (4-ounce) boneless,
  skinless chicken breasts

Chicken seasoning or rub

Salt

Pepper

Cooking oil

1 teaspoon paprika

To make the filling

1. In a small, microwave-safe bowl, heat the cream cheese in the microwave for 15 seconds to soften.

2. In a medium bowl, combine the cream cheese and the chopped spinach. Stir well. Set aside.

To make the chicken

1. Cut 4 or 5 slits into each chicken breast, without cutting all the way through.

2. Season the chicken with chicken seasoning, salt, and pepper to taste.

3. Spray the air fryer basket with cooking oil.

4. Place the chicken (with the slits facing up) in the air fryer. Do not stack. Cook in batches. Spray the chicken with cooking oil. Cook for 7 minutes.

5. Open the air fryer and stuff the spinach and cream cheese mixture into the slits of the chicken. Sprinkle ½ teaspoon of paprika all over the stuffed chicken breasts. Cook for an additional 3 minutes.

6. Remove the cooked chicken from the air fryer, then repeat steps 4 and 5 for the remaining chicken breasts.

7. Cool before serving.

Variation tip: If you have olives in your pantry, they make a lovely addition to this dish. Slice them and add to your spinach and cream cheese filling for a tangy flavor note.

Ingredient tip: Check the label to make sure your chicken seasoning is gluten-free.

Per serving: Calories: 192; Total fat: 9g; Saturated fat: 4g; Cholesterol: 86mg; Sodium: 201mg; Carbohydrates: 1g; Fiber: 0g; Protein: 28g

Low-Carb Naked Chicken Wings

FAST, FAMILY FAVORITE, GLUTEN-FREE

FRY: 400°F • PREP TIME: 10 MINUTES • COOK TIME: 15 MINUTES • SERVES 4

I love breaded, fried chicken wings just as much as the next person. However, you have to switch it up from time to time! Here, I stripped the breading, which lets the flavor of the chicken and seasonings shine. The absence of breading makes this recipe gluten-free and a *lot* lower in carbs.

8 whole chicken wings

1 teaspoon garlic powder

Chicken seasoning or rub

Pepper

Cooking oil

1. Season the wings with the garlic powder and chicken seasoning and pepper to taste.

2. Place the chicken wings in the air fryer. It is okay to stack them on top of each other. Spray the chicken with cooking oil. Cook for 10 minutes.

3. Remove the basket and shake it to ensure all of the chicken pieces will cook fully.

4. Return the basket and cook the chicken for an additional 5 minutes.

5. Cool before serving.

Variation tip: You can also use just chicken drumettes for this recipe.

Ingredient tip: Check the label to make sure your chicken seasoning is gluten-free.

Per serving: Calories: 254; Total fat: 18g; Saturated fat: 5g; Cholesterol: 85mg; Sodium: 109mg; Carbohydrates: 0g; Fiber: 0g; Protein: 21g

Cajun Chicken Drumsticks

FAMILY FAVORITE, GLUTEN-FREE

FRY: 390°F • PREP TIME: 5 MINUTES • COOK TIME: 40 MINUTES • SERVES 5

Who needs breading when the crispy chicken skin carries immense flavor? These low-carb drumsticks are liberally seasoned with Cajun seasoning—a versatile blend with a spicy kick. For a less spicy version of this recipe, I recommend using Tony Chachere's Creole Seasoning.

10 chicken drumsticks

1½ tablespoons Louisiana
   Cajun Seasoning

Salt

Pepper

Cooking oil

1. Season the drumsticks with the Cajun seasoning and salt and pepper to taste.

2. Spray the air fryer basket with cooking oil.

3. Place 5 drumsticks in the air fryer. Do not stack. Spray the drumsticks with cooking oil. Cook for 10 minutes.

4. Open the air fryer and flip the chicken. Cook for an additional 8 minutes.

5. Remove the cooked chicken from the air fryer, then repeat steps 3 and 4 for the remaining 5 drumsticks.

6. Cool before serving.

Ingredient tip: You can make your own Cajun seasoning using the following: 1 teaspoon paprika, ½ teaspoon onion powder, ½ teaspoon garlic powder, ½ teaspoon dried oregano, ½ teaspoon dried basil, ¼ teaspoon dried thyme, and ¼ teaspoon cayenne pepper.

Per serving: Calories: 253; Total fat: 17g; Saturated fat: 5g; Cholesterol: 114mg; Sodium: 391mg; Carbohydrates: 0g; Fiber: 0g; Protein: 25g

Cilantro-Lime Chicken

FAMILY FAVORITE, GLUTEN-FREE

BAKE: 400°F • PREP TIME: 5 MINUTES, PLUS 30 MINUTES TO MARINATE • COOK TIME: 20 MINUTES • SERVES 4

Simple, satisfying, light, low-carb, and gluten-free, Cilantro-Lime Chicken ticks a lot of boxes. I like to prep the chicken in the morning so it marinates all day and I can just pop it in the air fryer for a quick dinner. This is a dish the whole family will love. You will need a sealable plastic bag for this recipe.

4 (4-ounce) boneless, skinless chicken breasts

Chicken seasoning or rub

Salt

Pepper

½ cup chopped fresh cilantro

Juice of 1 lime

Cooking oil

1. Season the chicken with the chicken seasoning, salt, and pepper to taste.

2. Place the chicken in a sealable plastic bag. Add the cilantro and lime juice.

3. Marinate the chicken in the refrigerator for 30 minutes or up to 8 hours.

4. When ready to cook, spray the air fryer basket with cooking oil.

5. Place the chicken in the air fryer. Do not stack. Cook in batches. Spray the chicken with cooking oil. Cook for 7 minutes.

6. Open the air fryer and flip the chicken. Cook for an additional 3 minutes.

7. Remove the cooked chicken from the air fryer, then repeat steps 5 and 6 for the remaining chicken breasts.

8. Cool before serving.

Ingredient tip: Check the label to make sure your chicken seasoning is gluten-free.

Per serving: Calories: 122; Total fat: 2g; Saturated fat: 0g; Cholesterol: 65mg; Sodium: 138mg; Carbohydrates: 0g; Fiber: 0g; Protein: 26g

Ginger-Soy Glazed Chicken

FAST, FAMILY FAVORITE

BAKE: 400°F • PREP TIME: 5 MINUTES • COOK TIME: 20 MINUTES • SERVES 4

Many similar recipes use Asian specialty ingredients that aren't in everyone's pantries. Here, we strip it down to simple ingredients you might likely have on hand or which are available at most supermarkets. The magic in this dish lies in how bold the flavors are given the few, basic ingredients needed. I recommend serving Ginger-Soy Glazed Chicken on a bed of rice with a side of steamed broccoli.

4 (4-ounce) boneless, skinless chicken breasts

Chicken seasoning or rub

Salt

Pepper

Cooking oil

2 teaspoons grated fresh ginger

2 garlic cloves, minced

¼ cup honey

2 tablespoons soy sauce

1. Season the chicken with chicken seasoning, salt, and pepper to taste.
2. Spray the air fryer basket with cooking oil.
3. Place the chicken in the air fryer. Do not stack. Cook in batches. Spray the chicken with cooking oil. Cook for 7 minutes.
4. Open the air fryer and flip the chicken. Cook for an additional 3 minutes.
5. Remove the cooked chicken from the air fryer, then repeat steps 3 and 4 for the remaining chicken breasts.
6. While the chicken cooks, heat the ginger, garlic, honey, and soy sauce in a saucepan over medium-high heat. Stir to combine. Cook for 3 to 4 minutes, until the sauce thickens.
7. Transfer the chicken to a serving dish. Drizzle the chicken with the ginger and soy glaze, and serve.

Variation tip: To make this recipe gluten-free, replace the soy sauce with tamari. You can find it in the same aisle as soy sauce in the grocery store. Be sure to check the label.

Ingredient tip: Grated fresh ginger, or ginger sold in jars in the produce section of the grocery store, works best. You can also use 1 teaspoon ground ginger instead, which can be found in the spice aisle.

Per serving: Calories: 278; Total fat: 8g; Saturated Fat: 0g; Cholesterol: 0mg; Sodium: 515mg; Carbohydrates: 24g; Fiber: 0g; Protein: 28g

Barbecued Baby Back Ribs, page 141

CHAPTER 8

Beef, Pork, and Lamb

Rosemary Lamb Chops

FAST, FAMILY FAVORITE, GLUTEN-FREE

ROAST: 390°F • PREP TIME: 5 MINUTES • COOK TIME: 15 MINUTES • SERVES 4

With the air fryer, lamb chops aren't just something special you order when dining out—you can enjoy gourmet meals at home in 20 minutes flat. Pair these decadent lamb chops with your favorite red wine and Roasted Brown Butter Carrots (page 85).

8 (3-ounce) lamb chops

2 teaspoons extra-virgin olive oil

1½ teaspoons chopped fresh rosemary

1 garlic clove, minced

Salt

Pepper

1. Drizzle the lamb chops with olive oil.

2. In a small bowl, combine the rosemary, garlic, and salt and pepper to taste. Rub the seasoning onto the front and back of each lamb chop.

3. Place the lamb chops in the air fryer. It is okay to stack them. Cook for 10 minutes.

4. Open the air fryer. Flip the lamb chops. Cook for an additional 5 minutes.

5. Cool before serving.

Cooking tip: Use a meat thermometer to determine doneness using the following guidelines (before any resting time): 145°F for medium-rare, 160°F for medium, and 170°F for well-done.

Per serving: Calories: 308; Total fat: 17g; Saturated fat: 6g; Cholesterol: 113mg; Sodium: 159mg; Carbohydrates: 1g; Fiber: 0g; Protein: 35g

Panko-Breaded Pork Chops

FAST, FAMILY FAVORITE

FRY: 380°F • PREP TIME: 5 MINUTES • COOK TIME: 15 MINUTES • SERVES 5

Deep-fried pork chops are sometimes dry and tough. These air-fried pork chops retain their moist, juicy center with a crunchy, panko-breaded exterior. Pair with Crispy Brussels Sprouts (page 71) and Garlic-Roasted Red Potatoes (page 75) for an elegant meal.

5 (3½- to 5-ounce) pork chops (bone-in or boneless)

Seasoning salt

Pepper

¼ cup all-purpose flour

2 tablespoons panko bread crumbs

Cooking oil

1. Season the pork chops with the seasoning salt and pepper to taste.
2. Sprinkle the flour on both sides of the pork chops, then coat both sides with panko bread crumbs.
3. Place the pork chops in the air fryer. Stacking them is okay. (See Air fryer cooking tip.) Spray the pork chops with cooking oil. Cook for 6 minutes.
4. Open the air fryer and flip the pork chops. Cook for an additional 6 minutes
5. Cool before serving.

Ingredient tip: Typically, bone-in pork chops are juicier than boneless. If you prefer really juicy pork chops, use bone-in.

Cooking tip: Use a meat thermometer to determine doneness. A temperature of 145°F, plus 3 minutes of rest time, will result in medium pork chops that are safe to eat after resting. For well-done pork chops, remove the them at 160°F.

Air fryer cooking tip: Stacking the pork chops in the air fryer is okay. My preference is to cook 2 or 3 pork chops at a time without stacking them. This ensures each pork chop retains its breading as it cooks.

Per serving: Calories: 245; Total fat: 13g; Saturated fat: 5g; Cholesterol: 54mg; Sodium: 464mg; Carbohydrates: 6g; Fiber: 0g; Protein: 26g

Italian Parmesan Breaded Pork Chops

FAST, FAMILY FAVORITE

FRY: 380°F • PREP TIME: 5 MINUTES • COOK TIME: 25 MINUTES • SERVES 5

I grew up eating pork chops often. I feel like at least once every two weeks we would have fried pork chops, white rice with butter and sugar, and green beans. Those fried pork chops got so boring. No more boring pork chops! This lightened-up version packs a lot of flavor that your family will love. These pork chops are flavored and breaded with Italian seasoning, bread crumbs, and spices, all available at your local grocer. You won't need to travel as far as Italy to prepare this amazing dish.

5 (3½- to 5-ounce) pork chops (bone-in or boneless)

1 teaspoon Italian seasoning

Seasoning salt

Pepper

¼ cup all-purpose flour

2 tablespoons Italian bread crumbs

3 tablespoons finely grated Parmesan cheese

Cooking oil

1. Season the pork chops with the Italian seasoning and seasoning salt and pepper to taste.
2. Sprinkle the flour on both sides of the pork chops, then coat both sides with the bread crumbs and Parmesan cheese.
3. Place the pork chops in the air fryer. Stacking them is okay. (See Air fryer cooking tip.) Spray the pork chops with cooking oil. Cook for 6 minutes.
4. Open the air fryer and flip the pork chops. Cook for an additional 6 minutes.
5. Cool before serving.

Substitution tip: Instead of seasoning salt, you can use either chicken or pork rub for additional flavor. You can find these rubs in the spice aisle of the grocery store.

Ingredient tip: Typically, bone-in pork chops are juicier than boneless. If you prefer really juicy pork chops, use bone-in.

Cooking tip: Use a meat thermometer to determine doneness. A temperature of 145°F, plus 3 minutes of rest time, will result in medium pork chops that are safe to eat after resting. For well-done pork chops, remove them at 160°F.

Air fryer cooking tip: Stacking the pork chops in the air fryer is okay. My preference is to cook 2 or 3 pork chops at a time without stacking them. This ensures each pork chop retains its breading as it cooks.

Per serving: Calories: 334; Total fat: 18g; Saturated fat: 7g; Cholesterol: 75mg; Sodium: 665mg; Carbohydrates: 8g; Fiber: 0g; Protein: 34g

Sausage, Peppers, and Onions

FAST, FAMILY FAVORITE

FRY: 360°F • PREP TIME: 5 MINUTES • COOK TIME: 15 MINUTES • SERVES 5

These sizzling air-fried sausages are served on an Italian roll with tender-cooked peppers and onions. For this recipe, you can use fresh Italian sausages from a butcher or deli counter, or packaged sausages found in the self-serve area of a grocery store.

5 Italian sausages

1 green bell pepper, seeded and cut into strips

1 red bell pepper, seeded and cut into strips

½ onion, cut into strips

1 teaspoon dried oregano

½ teaspoon garlic powder

5 Italian rolls or buns

1. Place the sausages in the air fryer. No cooking oil is needed as the sausages will produce oil during the cooking process. The sausages should fit in the basket without stacking. If not, stacking is okay. Cook for 10 minutes.

2. Season the green and red bell peppers and the onion with the oregano and garlic powder.

3. Open the air fryer and flip the sausages. Add the peppers and onion to the basket. Cook for an additional 3 to 5 minutes, until the vegetables are soft and the sausages are no longer pink on the inside.

4. Serve the sausages (sliced or whole) on buns with the peppers and onion.

Air fryer cooking tip: You can line the air fryer basket with foil if your vegetables are thinly sliced. This will prevent the vegetable slices from falling below. Thick-sliced vegetables should be fine to place directly in the basket.

Per serving: Calories: 453; Total fat: 31g; Saturated fat: 11g; Cholesterol: 69mg; Sodium: 873mg; Carbohydrates: 26g; Fiber: 2g; Protein: 18g

Korean Short Ribs

FAMILY FAVORITE

BAKE/GRILL: 380°F • PREP TIME: 5 MINUTES, PLUS 1 HOUR TO MARINATE • COOK TIME: 10 MINUTES • SERVES 4

Korean-style short ribs are sweet, spicy, and fall-off-the-bone tender. The ribs are marinated in liquids and seasonings to produce juicy meat that is unbelievably succulent. You will need a sealable plastic bag for this recipe.

8 (8-ounce) bone-in short ribs

½ cup soy sauce

¼ cup rice wine vinegar (see Substitution tip)

½ cup chopped onion

2 garlic cloves, minced

1 tablespoon sesame oil

1 teaspoon Sriracha

4 scallions, green parts (white parts optional), thinly sliced, divided

Salt

Pepper

1. Place the short ribs in a sealable plastic bag. Add the soy sauce, rice wine vinegar, onion, garlic, sesame oil, Sriracha, and half of the scallions. Season with salt and pepper to taste.

2. Seal the bag and place it in the refrigerator to marinate for at least 1 hour; overnight is optimal.

3. Place the short ribs in the air fryer. Do not overfill. You may have to cook in two batches. Cook for 4 minutes.

4. Open the air fryer and flip the ribs. Cook for an additional 4 minutes.

5. If necessary, remove the cooked short ribs from the air fryer, then repeat steps 3 and 4 for the remaining ribs.

6. Sprinkle the short ribs with the remaining scallions, and serve.

Substitution tip: A tablespoon of brown sugar can be substituted for rice wine vinegar.

Ingredient tip: Korean-style short ribs (which are not the same as American and European-style short ribs) can be found at most Asian markets. The cut is also known as "flanken."

Cooking tip: Poke a knife or fork in the rib meat to check for doneness. If the knife slides in easily, the meat is tender and the ribs have finished cooking.

Per serving: Calories: 560; Total fat: 35g; Saturated fat: 15g; Cholesterol: 172mg; Sodium: 111mg; Carbohydrates: 0g; Fiber: 0g; Protein: 58g

Beef Taco Chimichangas

FAST, FAMILY FAVORITE

FRY: 400°F • PREP TIME: 10 MINUTES • COOK TIME: 20 MINUTES • SERVES 4

Basically burritos stuffed with meat, cheese, and sometimes rice, chimichangas served in restaurants are deep-fried and laden with grease. While super tasty, they are definitely not a healthy option. The air fryer cuts the fat, and dinner is ready in less than 30 minutes. Serve alongside rice and beans for a substantial meal.

Cooking oil

½ cup chopped onion

2 garlic cloves, minced

1 pound 93% lean ground beef

2 tablespoons taco seasoning

Salt

Pepper

1 (15-ounce) can diced tomatoes with chiles

4 medium (8-inch) flour tortillas

1 cup shredded Cheddar cheese (a blend of ½ cup shredded Cheddar and ½ cup shredded Monterey Jack works great, too)

1. Spray a skillet with cooking oil and place over medium-high heat. Add the chopped onion and garlic. Cook for 2 to 3 minutes, until fragrant.

2. Add the ground beef, taco seasoning, and salt and pepper to taste. Use a large spoon or spatula to break up the beef. Cook for 2 to 4 minutes, until browned.

3. Add the diced tomatoes with chiles. Stir to combine.

4. Mound ½ cup of the ground beef mixture on each of the tortillas.

5. To form the chimichangas, fold the sides of the tortilla in toward the middle and then roll up from the bottom. You can secure the chimichanga with a toothpick. Or you can moisten the upper edge of the tortilla with a small amount of water before sealing. I prefer to use a cooking brush, but you can dab with your fingers.

6. Spray the chimichangas with cooking oil.

7. Place the chimichangas in the air fryer. Do not stack. Cook in batches. Cook for 8 minutes.

AREN'T YOU GLAD YOU DIDN'T DEEP-FRY?

The air fryer saves you 10 grams of fat per serving compared to deep-frying.

8. Remove the cooked chimichangas from the air fryer and top them with the shredded cheese. The heat from the chimichangas will melt the cheese.

9. Repeat steps 7 and 8 for the remaining chimichangas, and serve.

Ingredient tips:

> Using 93% lean ground beef saves calories and fat. I can't tell any difference in taste!

> You can make your own taco seasoning by combining 1 teaspoon chili powder, 1 teaspoon cumin, ¼ teaspoon onion powder, ¼ teaspoon dried oregano, and ¼ teaspoon paprika.

Per serving: Calories: 558; Total fat: 38g; Saturated fat: 17g; Cholesterol: 115mg; Sodium: 1056mg; Carbohydrates: 22g; Fiber: 3g; Protein: 28g

BRANDI'S FAVORITE

★

Juicy Cheeseburgers

FAST, FAMILY FAVORITE

BAKE/GRILL: 360°F • PREP TIME: 5 MINUTES
COOK TIME: 15 MINUTES • SERVES 4

I was surprised to discover that burgers cook up nicely in the air fryer. It's quick and there's less mess than frying them in a pan. Why not load your cheeseburgers up with your favorite toppings? My favorites include sliced avocado, lettuce, tomatoes—and bacon. Pair this burger with Classic French Fries (see page 44) or your favorite seasoned frozen fries for an at-home fast-food treat.

1 pound 93% lean ground beef

1 teaspoon Worcestershire sauce

1 tablespoon burger seasoning

Salt

Pepper

Cooking oil

4 slices cheese

4 buns

1. In a large bowl, mix the ground beef, Worcestershire, burger seasoning, and salt and pepper to taste until well blended.

2. Spray the air fryer basket with cooking oil. You will need only a quick spritz. The burgers will produce oil as they cook.

3. Shape the mixture into 4 patties. Place the burgers in the air fryer. The burgers should fit without the need to stack, but stacking is okay if necessary. Cook for 8 minutes.

4. Open the air fryer and flip the burgers. Cook for an additional 3 to 4 minutes.

5. Check the inside of the burgers to determine if they have finished cooking. You can stick a knife or fork in the center to examine the color.

6. Top each burger with a slice of cheese. Cook for an additional minute, or until the cheese has melted.

7. Serve on buns with any additional toppings of your choice.

Ingredient tip: You can make your own burger seasoning using 1 teaspoon each of garlic powder, onion powder, and sugar.

Cooking tip: Cook time will vary depending on your desired doneness. You can stick a knife or fork in the center to determine the level of pink. You can also use a meat thermometer and cook to 125°F for rare, 135°F for medium-rare, 145°F for medium, 155°F for medium-well, and 160°F for well-done.

Air fryer cooking tip: You can toast your bun in the air fryer, too! Place the buns in the air fryer on 360°F for 2 to 3 minutes, until toasted.

Per serving: Calories: 566; Total fat: 39g; Saturated fat: 17g; Cholesterol: 114mg; Sodium: 535mg; Carbohydrates: 22g; Fiber: 1g; Protein: 29g

Beef and Cheese Empanadas

FAMILY FAVORITE

FRY: 400°F • PREP TIME: 15 MINUTES • COOK TIME: 25 MINUTES
MAKES 15 EMPANADAS (1 EMPANADA = 1 SERVING)

Getting your protein in a convenient, flaky little pocket is always a special treat. When you serve these air-fried empanadas for dinner, your whole family will be on board. Loaded with beef and cheese, the leftovers make a great lunch on the run. I dare you to eat just one!

Cooking oil

2 garlic cloves, chopped

⅓ cup chopped green bell pepper

⅓ medium onion, chopped

8 ounces 93% lean ground beef

1 teaspoon burger seasoning

Salt

Pepper

15 empanada wrappers

1 cup shredded mozzarella cheese

1 cup shredded Pepper Jack cheese

1 tablespoon butter

1. Spray a skillet with cooking oil and place over medium-high heat. Add the garlic, green bell pepper, and onion. Cook until fragrant, about 2 minutes.

2. Add the ground beef to the skillet. Season the beef with the hamburger seasoning and salt and pepper to taste. Using a spatula, break up the beef into small pieces. Cook the beef until browned. Drain any excess fat.

3. Lay the empanada wrappers on a flat surface.

4. Dip a basting brush in water. Glaze each of the empanada wrappers with the wet brush along the edges. This will soften the crust and make it easier to roll. You can also dip your fingers in water to moisten the edges.

5. Scoop 2 to 3 tablespoons of ground beef mixture onto each empanada wrapper. Sprinkle the mozzarella and Pepper Jack cheeses over the beef mixture.

6. Close the empanadas by folding the empanada in half. Using the back of a fork, press along the edges to seal.

7. Place 7 or 8 of the empanadas in the air fryer. Spray each with cooking oil. Cook for 8 minutes.

8. Open the air fryer and flip the empanadas. Cook for an additional 4 minutes.

9. Remove the cooked empanadas from the air fryer, then repeat steps 7 and 8 for the remaining 7 or 8 empanadas.

10. For added flavor, melt the butter in the microwave for 20 seconds. Using a cooking brush, spread the melted butter over the top of each.

11. Cool before serving.

Ingredient tip: Goya makes empanada wrappers that are usually available in the freezer section of the grocery store. If you can't find them, you can easily use egg roll wrappers instead.

Per serving: Calories: 173; Total fat: 7g; Saturated fat: 1g; Cholesterol: 14mg; Sodium: 164mg; Carbohydrates: 24g; Fiber: 0g; Protein: 7g

Ham and Cheese Stromboli

FAST, FAMILY FAVORITE

FRY: 400°F • PREP TIME: 10 MINUTES • COOK TIME: 20 MINUTES
MAKES 6 STROMBOLI (1 STROMBOLI = 1 SERVING)

Allegedly originating from Italian immigrants in Philadelphia, a stromboli is a savory turnover that is filled with melted cheese, deli meat, and vegetables. Think ham and cheese sandwich meets pizza. This air-fried rendition will definitely upgrade your typical lunch.

1 teaspoon all-purpose flour

1 (13-ounce) can refrigerated pizza dough

6 slices provolone cheese

½ cup shredded mozzarella cheese

12 slices deli ham

½ red bell pepper, seeded and sliced

½ teaspoon dried basil

½ teaspoon oregano

Pepper

Cooking oil

1. Sprinkle the flour on a flat work surface. Roll out the pizza dough. Cut the dough into 6 equal-sized rectangles.

2. Add 1 slice of provolone, 1 tablespoon of mozzarella, 2 slices of ham, and a few slices of red bell pepper to each of the rectangles.

3. Season each with dried basil, oregano, and pepper to taste.

4. Fold up each crust to close the stromboli. Using the back of a fork, press along the open edges to seal.

5. Place the stromboli in the air fryer. Do not stack. Cook in batches. Spray the stromboli with cooking oil. Cook for 10 minutes.

6. Remove the cooked stromboli from the air fryer, then repeat step 5 for the remaining stromboli.

7. Cool before serving.

Variation tip: Sprinkle a teaspoon of Italian seasoning or ½ teaspoon basil and ½ teaspoon oregano on top of the stromboli before baking for added flavor.

Cooking tip: Check in on the stromboli after 7 to 8 minutes to ensure they are not too crisp for your liking. Cook until they turn golden brown.

Per serving: Calories: 362; Total fat: 15g; Saturated fat: 7g; Cholesterol: 52mg; Sodium: 1460mg; Carbohydrates: 35g; Fiber: 2g; Protein: 22g

Beef and Mushroom Calzones

FAST, FAMILY FAVORITE

FRY: 400°F • PREP TIME: 10 MINUTES • COOK TIME: 20 MINUTES
MAKES 6 CALZONES (1 CALZONE = 1 SERVING)

These calzones are a lot like pizza rolls. Italian seasoned ground beef is packed inside warm pizza crust along with melted cheese. You can even mix it up depending on what you have in your refrigerator and pantry. For example, exchange the ground beef for pepperoni if you wish, or use your favorite cheese; the variations are endless.

Cooking oil

½ cup chopped onion

2 garlic cloves, minced

¼ cup chopped mushrooms

1 pound 93% lean ground beef

1 tablespoon Italian seasoning

Salt

Pepper

1½ cups pizza sauce

1 teaspoon all-purpose flour

1 (13-ounce) can refrigerated pizza dough

1 cup shredded Cheddar cheese

1. Spray a skillet with cooking oil and place over medium-high heat. Add the chopped onion, garlic, and mushrooms. Cook for 2 to 3 minutes, until fragrant.

2. Add the ground beef, Italian seasoning, and salt and pepper to taste. Use a large spoon or spatula to break up the beef into small pieces. Cook for 2 to 4 minutes, until browned.

3. Add the pizza sauce. Stir to combine.

4. Sprinkle the flour on a flat work surface. Roll out the pizza dough. Cut the dough into 6 equal-sized rectangles.

5. Mound ½ cup of the ground beef mixture on each of the rectangles. Sprinkle 1 tablespoon of shredded cheese over the beef mixture.

6. Fold each crust up to close the calzones. Using the back of a fork, press along the open edges of each calzone to seal.

7. Place the calzones in the air fryer. Do not stack. Cook in batches. Spray the calzones with cooking oil. Cook for 10 minutes.

8. Remove the cooked calzones from the air fryer, then repeat step 7 for the remaining calzones.

9. Cool before serving.

Cooking tip: Check in on the calzones after 7 to 8 minutes to ensure they are not too crisp for your liking. Cook until they turn golden brown.

Per serving: Calories: 303; Total fat: 12g; Saturated fat: 6g; Cholesterol: 36mg; Sodium: 689mg; Carbohydrates: 35g; Fiber: 2g; Protein: 15g

Sizzling Beef Fajitas

FAST, FAMILY FAVORITE

ROAST/GRILL: 380°F • PREP TIME: 10 MINUTES • COOK TIME: 10 MINUTES • SERVES 4

A decked-out dish of fajitas feels like an indulgent restaurant meal, but with the air fryer, you can enjoy them at home in less than a half hour, for a fraction of the cost. These juicy fajitas are made up of steak, peppers, and onions served sizzling hot with flour tortillas. Be sure to add your favorite toppings, like sour cream, guacamole, and salsa.

1 pound beef flank steak, cut into strips

1 red bell pepper, cut into strips

1 green bell pepper, cut into strips

½ red onion, cut into strips

2 tablespoons taco or fajita seasoning

Salt

Pepper

2 tablespoons extra-virgin olive oil

8 medium (8-inch) flour tortillas

1. In a large bowl, combine the beef, red and green bell peppers, onion, taco seasoning, salt and pepper to taste, and olive oil. Mix well.

2. Transfer the beef and vegetable mixture to the air fryer. It is okay to stack. Cook for 5 minutes.

3. Open the air fryer and shake the basket. Cook for an additional 4 to 5 minutes.

4. Divide the beef and vegetables evenly among the tortillas and serve with any of your desired additional toppings.

Ingredient tip: You can make your own taco seasoning using the following: 1 teaspoon chili powder, 1 teaspoon cumin, ¼ teaspoon onion powder, ¼ teaspoon dried oregano, and ¼ teaspoon paprika.

Cooking tip: Cook time will vary depending on your desired doneness. Check the inside of the meat to determine if it is cooked to your liking. You can stick a knife or fork in the center to review the level of pink. You can also use a meat thermometer and cook to 125°F for rare, 135°F for medium-rare, 145°F for medium, 155°F for medium-well, and 160°F for well-done.

Air fryer cooking tip: You can line the air fryer basket with foil if your vegetables are thinly sliced. This will prevent the vegetable slices from falling below. Thick-sliced vegetables should be fine to place directly into the basket.

Per serving: Calories: 378; Total fat: 16g; Saturated fat: 4g; Cholesterol: 50mg; Sodium: 389mg; Carbohydrates: 30g; Fiber: 4g; Protein: 28g

Roasted Pork Tenderloin

FAMILY FAVORITE, GLUTEN-FREE

For special occasions, this Roasted Pork Tenderloin is impressive. But this recipe is simple enough that it can also be prepared on a Wednesday for dinner. The finished tenderloin is succulent and bursting with flavor. Pair with mashed potatoes and a side salad for a satisfying air fryer meal.

1 (3-pound) pork tenderloin

2 tablespoons extra-virgin olive oil

2 garlic cloves, minced

1 teaspoon dried basil

1 teaspoon dried oregano

1 teaspoon dried thyme

Salt

Pepper

1. Drizzle the pork tenderloin with the olive oil.
2. Rub the garlic, basil, oregano, thyme, and salt and pepper to taste all over the tenderloin.
3. Place the tenderloin in the air fryer. Cook for 45 minutes.
4. Use a meat thermometer to test for doneness. (See Cooking tip.)
5. Open the air fryer and flip the pork tenderloin. Cook for an additional 15 minutes.
6. Remove the cooked pork from the air fryer and allow it to rest for 10 minutes before cutting.

Cooking tip: Use a meat thermometer to test for doneness. The pork loin should have an internal temperature between 145°F (medium-rare) and 160°F (medium).

Per serving: Calories: 283; Total fat: 10g; Saturated fat: 3g; Cholesterol: 150mg; Sodium: 147mg; Carbohydrates: 1g; Fiber: 0g; Protein: 48g

Beef Ribeye Steak

FAST, FAMILY FAVORITE, GLUTEN-FREE

ROAST/GRILL: 360°F • PREP TIME: 5 MINUTES • COOK TIME: 20 MINUTES • SERVES 4

I am a midwestern girl who loves to grill. Sometimes our winters are so harsh, I can't even get to my grill on the patio because it's buried in snow! Did you know you can make steak in the air fryer? It produces mouthwateringly juicy steaks without any added oil.

4 (8-ounce) ribeye steaks

1 tablespoon McCormick Grill Mates Montreal Steak Seasoning

Salt

Pepper

1. Season the steaks with the steak seasoning and salt and pepper to taste.

2. Place 2 steaks in the air fryer. You can use an accessory grill pan, a layer rack, or the standard air fryer basket. Cook for 4 minutes.

3. Open the air fryer and flip the steaks. Cook for an additional 4 to 5 minutes.

4. Check for doneness to determine how much additional cook time is need. (See Cooking tip.)

5. Remove the cooked steaks from the air fryer, then repeat steps 2 through 4 for the remaining 2 steaks.

6. Cool before serving.

Ingredient tip: You can make your own steak rub using the following: 1 teaspoon onion powder, 1 teaspoon garlic powder, 1 teaspoon paprika, and 1 teaspoon coriander.

Prep tip: You can dry marinate the steaks in the seasonings in sealable plastic bags in the refrigerator overnight. This will produce a more flavorful and juicy steak.

Cooking tip: Cook time will vary depending on your desired doneness. Check the inside of the meat to determine if it is cooked to your liking. You can stick a knife or fork in the center to review the level of pink. You can also use a meat thermometer and cook to 125°F for rare, 135°F for medium-rare, 145°F for medium, 155°F for medium-well, and 160°F for well-done.

Per serving: Calories: 293; Total fat: 22g; Saturated fat: 11g; Cholesterol: 71mg; Sodium: 519mg; Carbohydrates: 0g; Fiber: 0g; Protein: 23g

Swedish Meatballs

FAST, FAMILY FAVORITE

BAKE/ROAST: 370°F • PREP TIME: 10 MINUTES • COOK TIME: 20 MINUTES
MAKES 10 MEATBALLS (1 MEATBALL = 1 SERVING

With this recipe, you won't have to run to IKEA for Swedish meatballs. Drizzled in gravy, this dish is quick and easy to whip up in the air fryer. These meatballs are hearty in size. I typically eat two or three meatballs at a sitting. If you plan to prepare them for children, you may consider making them smaller.

For the meatballs

1 pound 93% lean
   ground beef

1 (1-ounce) packet Lipton
   Onion Recipe Soup
   & Dip Mix

⅓ cup bread crumbs

1 egg, beaten

Salt

Pepper

For the gravy

1 cup beef broth

⅓ cup heavy cream

2 tablespoons all-
   purpose flour

To make the meatballs

1. In a large bowl, combine the ground beef, onion soup mix, bread crumbs, egg, and salt and pepper to taste. Mix thoroughly.

2. I recommend you use gloves to assemble the meatballs. Using 2 tablespoons of the meat mixture, create each meatball by rolling the beef mixture around in your hands. This should yield about 10 meatballs.

3. Place the meatballs in the air fryer. It is okay to stack them. Cook for 14 minutes.

To make the gravy

1. While the meatballs cook, prepare the gravy. Heat a saucepan over medium-high heat.

2. Add the beef broth and heavy cream. Stir for 1 to 2 minutes.

3. Add the flour and stir. Cover and allow the sauce to simmer for 3 to 4 minutes, or until thick.

4. Drizzle the gravy over the meatballs and serve.

Substitution tip: You can substitute the Lipton soup mix with 2 tablespoons minced onion, ¼ teaspoon dried parsley, ⅛ teaspoon celery salt, and ½ teaspoon turmeric.

Per serving: Calories: 178; Total fat: 14g; Saturated fat: 6g; Cholesterol: 56mg; Sodium: 217mg; Carbohydrates: 4g; Fiber: 0g; Protein: 9g

Chicken-Fried Steak

FAST, FAMILY FAVORITE

FRY: 370°F • PREP TIME: 10 MINUTES • COOK TIME: 15 MINUTES • SERVES 4

Chicken-Fried Steak is a Southern classic and is prepared with white home-style country gravy. Many confuse this dish with poultry, but it's beef coated with the iconic crispy breading of fried chicken. Serve this dish with Garlic-Roasted Red Potatoes (page 75) and Vegetable Medley (page 77) for a balanced and filling meal.

For the steak

½ cup all-purpose flour

Seasoning salt

Pepper

Cooking oil

2 eggs

¾ cup panko bread crumbs

4 (4-ounce) cube steaks

For the gravy

1 (0.87-ounce) package McCormick Homestyle Country Gravy Mix (or other packaged white gravy mix)

2 cups water

To make the steak

1. In a bowl, combine the flour and seasoning salt and pepper to taste.

2. Spray the air fryer basket with cooking oil.

3. In a small bowl, beat the eggs. Add the panko to another bowl.

4. Dip each steak in the flour, then the eggs, and then the bread crumbs.

5. Place the steaks in the air fryer. Do not stack. Cook in batches. Spray the top of the steaks with cooking oil. Cook for 7 minutes.

6. Remove the cooked steaks from the air fryer, then repeat step 5 for the remaining steaks.

To make the gravy

1. While the steaks cook, prepare the gravy. Place a saucepan over medium heat. Add the gravy mix.

2. Slowly add water to the pan. Stir frequently until the mix boils. Reduce heat and simmer for 1 minute. The sauce will thicken upon standing. Drizzle the gravy over the steaks, and serve.

Substitution tip: Regular bread crumbs can be used if you don't have panko on hand.

Per serving: Calories: 297; Total fat: 10g; Saturated fat: 3g; Cholesterol: 157mg; Sodium: 369mg; Carbohydrates: 20g; Fiber: 2g; Protein: 31g

AREN'T YOU GLAD YOU DIDN'T DEEP-FRY?

Air fryer chicken-fried steak has 10 grams of fat per serving, compared to 27 grams when you deep-fry.

Barbecued Baby Back Ribs

FAMILY FAVORITE

BAKE/GRILL: 360°F • PREP TIME: 5 MINUTES, PLUS 30 MINUTES
TO DRY MARINATE • COOK TIME: 30 MINUTES • SERVES 4

I live in Kansas City, Missouri. Barbecue is our thing. Ribs are a *big* deal here. I am thrilled that I can still prepare my favorite ribs during the cold winter months using the air fryer. This recipe is loaded with flavor, and your ribs will turn out finger-licking good! Grab your favorite barbecue sauce and let's dig in.

1 rack baby back ribs

1 teaspoon onion powder

1 teaspoon garlic powder

1 teaspoon brown sugar

1 teaspoon dried oregano

Salt

Pepper

½ cup barbecue sauce

1. Use a sharp knife to remove the thin membrane from the back of the ribs. Cut the rack in half or as needed so that the ribs are able to fit in the air fryer.

2. In a small bowl, combine the onion powder, garlic powder, brown sugar, oregano, and salt and pepper to taste. Rub the seasoning onto the front and back of the ribs.

3. Cover the ribs with plastic wrap or foil and allow them to sit at room temperature for 30 minutes.

4. Place the ribs in the air fryer. It is okay to stack them. Cook for 15 minutes.

5. Open the air fryer. Flip the ribs. Cook for an additional 15 minutes.

6. Transfer the ribs to a serving dish. Drizzle the ribs with the barbecue sauce and serve.

Substitution tip: You can use a store-bought pork rub in place of the seasonings noted above.

Variation tip: Make this recipe gluten-free by using gluten-free barbecue sauce. Be sure to check the label.

Cooking tip: Using a knife or fork, poke the rib meat to check for doneness. If it slides in easily, the meat is tender and the ribs have finished cooking.

Per serving: Calories: 375; Total fat: 27g; Saturated fat: 10g; Cholesterol: 90mg; Sodium: 474mg; Carbohydrates: 13g; Fiber: 1g; Protein: 18g

Chocolate Donuts, page 150

CHAPTER 9

Dessert

Apple-Cinnamon Hand Pies

FAMILY FAVORITE, VEGETARIAN

FRY: 400°F • PREP TIME: 15 MINUTES • COOK TIME: 20 MINUTES
MAKES 8 HAND PIES (1 HAND PIE = 1 SERVING)

Replace your traditional slice of pie with these handheld pastries. Any kind of apples will work for this warm and flaky cinnamon treat. These are best served warm with a scoop of vanilla ice cream.

2 apples, cored and diced

¼ cup honey

1 teaspoon cinnamon

1 teaspoon vanilla extract

⅛ teaspoon nutmeg

2 teaspoons cornstarch

1 teaspoon water

4 frozen piecrusts, thawed if frozen hard

Cooking oil

1. Place a saucepan over medium-high heat. Add the apples, honey, cinnamon, vanilla, and nutmeg. Stir and cook for 2 to 3 minutes, until the apples are soft.

2. In a small bowl, mix the cornstarch and water. Add to the pan and stir. Cook for 30 seconds.

3. Cut each piecrust into two 4-inch circles. You should have 8 circles of crust total.

4. Lay the piecrusts on a flat work surface. Mound ⅓ cup of apple filling on the center of each.

5. Fold each piecrust over so that the top layer of crust is about an inch short of the bottom layer. (The edges should not meet.)

6. Using your fingers, tap along the edges of the top layer to seal. Use the back of a fork to press lines into the edges.

7. Place the hand pies in the air fryer. I do not recommend stacking the hand pies. They will stick together if stacked. You may need to prepare them in two batches. Cook for 10 minutes.

8. Allow the hand pies to cool fully before removing from the air fryer.

Cooking tip: Check in on the pies to monitor if the cook time needs adjustment. The pies will turn golden brown when complete.

Per serving: Calories: 493; Total fat: 21g; Saturated fat: 3g; Cholesterol: 0mg; Sodium: 410mg; Carbohydrates: 49g; Fiber: 2g; Protein: 3g

Cherry Turnovers

FAST, FAMILY FAVORITE, VEGETARIAN

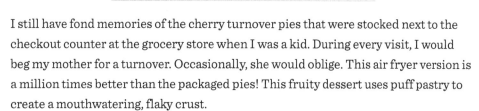

BAKE: 370°F • PREP TIME: 15 MINUTES • COOK TIME: 20 MINUTES
MAKES 8 TURNOVERS (1 TURNOVER = 1 SERVING)

I still have fond memories of the cherry turnover pies that were stocked next to the checkout counter at the grocery store when I was a kid. During every visit, I would beg my mother for a turnover. Occasionally, she would oblige. This air fryer version is a million times better than the packaged pies! This fruity dessert uses puff pastry to create a mouthwatering, flaky crust.

1 (17-ounce) box frozen puff pastry dough, thawed (see Prep tip)

1 (10-ounce) can cherry pie filling

1 egg white, beaten

Cooking oil

1. Unfold both sheets of puff pastry dough and cut each into 4 squares for 8 squares total.

2. Spoon ½ to 1 tablespoon of cherry pie filling onto the center of each square. Do not overfill or the filling will leak out the turnover.

3. Use a cooking brush or your fingers to brush the edges of the squares with the egg white.

4. Fold the dough over diagonally to close each turnover. Using the back of a fork, press lines into the open edges of each turnover to seal.

5. Spray the air fryer basket with cooking oil.

6. Place the turnovers in the air fryer, being careful not to let them touch. Do not stack. Cook in batches. Spray the turnovers with cooking oil. Cook for 8 minutes.

7. Cool for 3 or 4 minutes before removing from the air fryer. The turnovers may stick to the basket if not cooled.

8. Repeat steps 6 and 7 for the remaining turnovers.

Prep tip: Thaw the puff pastry in the refrigerator at least 4 hours prior to preparing this recipe. You can also thaw at room temperature, but for no longer than 40 minutes. Don't thaw the pastry in the microwave.

Per serving: Calories: 224; Total fat: 12g; Saturated fat: 5g; Cholesterol: 0mg; Sodium: 136mg; Carbohydrates: 27g; Fiber: 1g; Protein: 4g

Pineapple Cream Cheese Wontons

FAMILY FAVORITE, VEGETARIAN

FRY: 380°F • PREP TIME: 5 MINUTES • COOK TIME: 40 MINUTES
MAKES 20 WONTONS (2 WONTONS = 1 SERVING)

If you are a fan of Crab Rangoon, this is the dessert for you. The wontons have a warm, flaky exterior and a creamy pineapple filling, perfect for indulging. Don't worry about the fat—the air fryer slashes it.

8 ounces cream cheese

1 cup finely chopped fresh pineapple (canned, drained pineapple can be used)

20 wonton wrappers

Cooking oil

> **AREN'T YOU GLAD YOU DIDN'T DEEP-FRY?**
>
> This recipe cuts 15 grams of fat by using the air fryer!

1. In a small, microwave-safe bowl, heat the cream cheese in the microwave for 20 seconds to soften.

2. In a medium bowl, combine the cream cheese and pineapple. Stir to mix well.

3. Lay out the wonton wrappers on a work surface. A clean table or large cutting board works well.

4. Spoon 1½ teaspoons of the cream cheese and pineapple mixture onto each wrapper. Be careful not to overfill.

5. Fold each wrapper diagonally across to form a triangle. Bring the 2 bottom corners up toward each other. Do not close the wrapper yet. Bring up the 2 open sides and push out any air. Squeeze the open edges together to seal.

6. Place the wontons in the air fryer and cook in batches, or stack (see Air fryer cooking tip). Spray with cooking oil. Cook for 10 minutes.

7. Remove the basket and flip each wonton. Return the basket to the air fryer. Cook the wontons for an additional 5 to 8 minutes, until they have reached your desired level of golden brown and crisp.

8. If cooking in batches, remove the cooked wontons from the air fryer, then repeat steps 6 and 7 for the remaining wontons.

9. Cool before serving.

Substitution tip: I prefer to use reduced-fat cream cheese. It helps keep the calories and fat content low, making it a bit friendlier to my waistline, and the difference in taste is imperceptible!

Cooking tip: Check in on the wontons throughout the cooking process to ensure the wontons do not overheat. The wontons have finished cooking when the color has reached a light golden brown. If the wontons overheat, the filling may leak.

Air fryer cooking tip: You can choose to stack the wontons throughout the air fryer or cook them in separate batches. The total cook time indicated (40 minutes) is for two batches. While stacking them is quicker, preparing the wontons in batches works best. If you stack them, you may have a few that are really soft and break apart when you try to flip them over.

Per serving: Calories: 137; Total fat: 9g; Saturated fat: 5g; Cholesterol: 27mg; Sodium: 164mg; Carbohydrates: 13g; Fiber: 1g; Protein: 4g

Cinnamon Crunch S'mores

FAST, FAMILY FAVORITE, VEGETARIAN

BAKE: 350°F • PREP TIME: 5 MINUTES • COOK TIME: 10 MINUTES
MAKES 12 S'MORES (1 S'MORE = 1 SERVING)

Campfire s'mores can now be made in the kitchen—and in a fraction of the time—with the help of the air fryer. This classic recipe is incredibly easy. Kids and adults alike gobble up this fun treat.

12 whole cinnamon graham crackers

2 (1.55-ounce) chocolate bars, broken into 12 pieces

12 marshmallows

1. Halve each graham cracker into 2 squares.
2. Place 6 graham cracker squares in the air fryer. Do not stack. Place a piece of chocolate onto each. Cook for 2 minutes.
3. Open the air fryer and add a marshmallow onto each piece of melted chocolate. Cook for 1 additional minute.
4. Remove the cooked s'mores from the air fryer, then repeat steps 2 and 3 for the remaining 6 s'mores.
5. Top with the remaining graham cracker squares and serve.

Cooking tip: For dark brown marshmallows, add the marshmallow on top of the chocolate in step 2 and cook together for 3 to 4 minutes.

Per serving: Calories: 112; Total fat: 3g; Saturated fat: 2g; Cholesterol: 0mg; Sodium: 93mg; Carbohydrates: 21g; Fiber: 1g; Protein: 1g

Strawberry Cheesecake Rolls

FAST, FAMILY FAVORITE, VEGETARIAN

BRANDI'S FAVORITE
★

FRY: 350°F • PREP TIME: 10 MINUTES • COOK TIME: 20 MINUTES
MAKES 12 ROLLS (1 ROLL = 1 SERVING)

When it comes to dessert, cheesecake wins my heart, *especially* when paired with strawberries. I crave a dessert that isn't overly rich, but is still loaded with flavor. These Strawberry Cheesecake Rolls fit the bill and pack a sweet punch into a small, bite-sized package.

1 (8-ounce) can crescent rolls

4 ounces cream cheese

1 tablespoon strawberry preserves

1/3 cup sliced fresh strawberries

Cooking oil

1. On a flat work surface, roll out the dough into a large rectangle.

2. Cut the dough into 12 rectangles by making 3 cuts crosswise and 2 cuts lengthwise.

3. Place the cream cheese in a small, microwave-safe bowl. Microwave for 15 seconds to soften.

4. In a medium bowl, combine the cream cheese and strawberry preserves and stir.

5. Scoop 2 teaspoons of the cream cheese and strawberry mixture onto each piece of dough. Spread, but avoid the edges of the dough.

6. Add 2 teaspoons of fresh strawberries to each.

7. Roll up each of the rectangles to create a roll.

8. Spray the air fryer basket with cooking oil.

9. Place the rolls in the basket. Do not stack. Cook in batches. Spray the rolls with cooking oil. Cook for 8 minutes.

10. Allow the rolls to cool for 2 to 3 minutes, then remove from the air fryer.

11. Repeat steps 9 and 10 for the remaining rolls.

12. Cool before serving.

Substitution tip: Reduced-fat cream cheese can be used as a substitute to save on calories and fat.

Cooking tip: Be sure to allow the rolls to cool before removing from the air fryer. The rolls will lose their shape if handled while hot.

Per serving: Calories: 98; Total fat: 5g; Saturated fat: 2g; Cholesterol: 11mg; Sodium: 130mg; Carbohydrates: 12g; Fiber: 1g; Protein: 3g

Chocolate Donuts

FAST, FAMILY FAVORITE, VEGETARIAN

FRY: 360°F • PREP TIME: 5 MINUTES • COOK TIME: 20 MINUTES
MAKES 8 DONUTS (1 DONUT = 1 SERVING)

Chocolate donuts are great for dessert—or even breakfast! Deep-fried bakery donuts are loaded with a ton of sugar and fat. These donuts are lightened up by air-frying, and you can make them quickly using everyday items on hand in your home.

1 (8-ounce) can jumbo biscuits

Cooking oil

Chocolate sauce, such as Hershey's

AREN'T YOU GLAD YOU DIDN'T DEEP-FRY?

Air-fried donuts save 8 grams of fat per serving in comparison to a chocolate donut from a bakery.

1. Separate the biscuit dough into 8 biscuits and place them on a flat work surface. Use a small circle cookie cutter or a biscuit cutter to cut a hole in the center of each biscuit. You can also cut the holes using a knife.

2. Spray the air fryer basket with cooking oil.

3. Place 4 donuts in the air fryer. Do not stack. Spray with cooking oil. Cook for 4 minutes.

4. Open the air fryer and flip the donuts. Cook for an additional 4 minutes.

5. Remove the cooked donuts from the air fryer, then repeat steps 3 and 4 for the remaining 4 donuts.

6. Drizzle chocolate sauce over the donuts and enjoy while warm. (For homemade chocolate sauce, see Ingredient tip in Fried Bananas with Chocolate Sauce, page 152.)

Ingredient tip: Don't let the biscuit rounds you cut out in step 1 go to waste! Use them to make Cinnamon Sugar Donut Holes (page 153).

Per serving: Calories: 181; Total fat: 8g; Saturated fat: 2g; Cholesterol: 0mg; Sodium: 460mg; Carbohydrates: 25g; Fiber: 1g; Protein: 3g

Blueberry Crisp

FAST, FAMILY FAVORITE, VEGETARIAN

BAKE: 350°F • PREP TIME: 5 MINUTES • COOK TIME: 15 MINUTES • SERVES 8

This recipe is so easy to make—simply combine all of the ingredients and let the air fryer do the rest of the work. A traditional blueberry crisp can take an hour to cook in the oven. This recipe is ready to enjoy in less than 30 minutes! You will need a barrel pan accessory for this recipe.

1 cup rolled oats

½ cup all-purpose flour

¼ cup extra-virgin olive oil

¼ teaspoon salt

1 teaspoon cinnamon

⅓ cup honey

Cooking oil

4 cups blueberries (thawed if frozen)

1. In a large bowl, combine the rolled oats, flour, olive oil, salt, cinnamon, and honey.

2. Spray a barrel pan with cooking oil all over the bottom and sides of the pan.

3. Spread the blueberries on the bottom of the barrel pan. Top with the oat mixture.

4. Place the pan in the air fryer. Cook for 15 minutes.

5. Cool before serving.

Ingredient tip: Blueberries are usually somewhat tart. If you prefer a sweeter dish, add 2 tablespoons sugar in step 1.

Per serving: Calories: 187; Total fat: 7g; Saturated fat: 1g; Cholesterol: 0mg; Sodium: 75mg; Carbohydrates: 32g; Fiber: 3g; Protein: 2g

Fried Bananas with Chocolate Sauce

FAST, FAMILY FAVORITE, VEGETARIAN

FRY: 350°F • PREP TIME: 10 MINUTES • COOK TIME: 10 MINUTES • SERVES 6

Here is a quick and easy dessert recipe that everyone in the family will enjoy. These fried bananas have a crunchy exterior with a gooey center. Your home will smell like dessert once you get the air fryer going. The drizzled chocolate sauce is just icing on the cake! I prefer to use bananas that are fully ripe, yellow with brown speckles, but still firm.

1 large egg

¼ cup cornstarch

¼ cup plain bread crumbs

3 bananas, halved
   crosswise

Cooking oil

Chocolate sauce (see
   Ingredient tip)

1. In a small bowl, beat the egg. In another bowl, place the cornstarch. Place the bread crumbs in a third bowl.

2. Dip the bananas in the cornstarch, then the egg, and then the bread crumbs.

3. Spray the air fryer basket with cooking oil.

4. Place the bananas in the basket and spray them with cooking oil. Cook for 5 minutes.

5. Open the air fryer and flip the bananas. Cook for an additional 2 minutes.

6. Transfer the bananas to plates. Drizzle the chocolate sauce over the bananas, and serve.

Ingredient tip: You can make your own chocolate sauce using 2 tablespoons milk and ¼ cup chocolate chips. Heat a saucepan over medium-high heat. Add the milk and stir for 1 to 2 minutes. Add the chocolate chips. Stir for 2 minutes, or until the chocolate has melted.

Per serving: Calories: 203; Total fat: 6g; Saturated fat: 4g; Cholesterol: 36mg; Sodium: 56mg; Carbohydrates: 33g; Fiber: 3g; Protein: 3g

Cinnamon Sugar Donut Holes

FAST, FAMILY FAVORITE, VEGETARIAN

FRY: 360°F • PREP TIME: 5 MINUTES • COOK TIME: 20 MINUTES
MAKES 16 DONUT HOLES (1 DONUT HOLE = 1 SERVING)

These donut holes make the perfect pop-in-your mouth snack. You can use the leftover dough from Chocolate Donuts (page 150) to make these donut holes.

1 (8-ounce) can jumbo biscuit dough

Cooking oil

1 tablespoon stevia

2 tablespoons cinnamon

1. Form the biscuit dough evenly into 16 balls, 1 to 1½ inches thick.

2. Spray the air fryer basket with cooking oil.

3. Place 8 donut holes in the air fryer. Do not stack. Spray them with cooking oil. Cook for 4 minutes.

4. Open the air fryer and flip the donut holes. Cook for an additional 4 minutes.

5. Remove the cooked donut holes, then repeat steps 3 and 4 for the remaining 8 donut holes. Allow the donut holes to cool.

6. In a small bowl, combine the stevia and cinnamon and stir.

7. Spritz the donut holes with cooking oil. Dip the donut holes in the cinnamon and sugar mixture, and serve.

Substitution tip: To use real sugar, replace the stevia with ¼ cup of sugar.

Per serving: Calories: 51; Total fat: 2g; Saturated fat: 1g; Cholesterol: 0mg; Sodium: 158mg; Carbohydrates: 8g; Fiber: 1g; Protein: 1g

Peanut Butter Banana Pastry Bites

FAMILY FAVORITE, VEGETARIAN

FRY: 375°F • PREP TIME: 5 MINUTES • COOK TIME: 40 MINUTES • MAKES 12 BITES (1 BITE = 1 SERVING)

The creaminess of peanut butter lends itself to desserts. And the fact that it's a high-protein ingredient helps balance out this air-fried treat. When combined with banana, it defines indulgence.

12 wonton wrappers

1 banana, cut into 12 pieces

½ cup peanut butter

Cooking oil

1. Lay out the wonton wrappers on a work surface. A clean table or large cutting board works well.

2. Place 1 banana slice and 1 teaspoon of peanut butter on each wrapper.

3. Fold each wrapper diagonally across to form a triangle. Bring the 2 bottom corners up toward each other. Do not close the wrapper yet. Bring up the 2 open sides and push out any air. Squeeze the open edges together to seal.

4. Spray the air fryer basket with cooking oil.

5. Place the bites in the air fryer basket and cook in batches, or stack (see Air fryer cooking tip). Spray with cooking oil. Cook for 10 minutes.

6. Remove the basket and flip each bite over.

7. Return the basket to the air fryer. Cook for an additional 5 to 8 minutes, until the bites have reached your desired level of golden brown and crisp.

8. If cooking in batches, remove the cooked bites from the air fryer, then repeat steps 5 through 7 for the remaining bites.

9. Cool before serving.

Cooking tip: Check in on the bites throughout the cooking process to ensure the bites do not overheat. The bites have finished cooking when the color has reached a light golden brown. If the bites overheat, the filling may leak.

Air fryer cooking tip: You can choose to stack the bites throughout the air fryer or cook them in separate batches. The total cook time indicated (40 minutes) is for two batches. While stacking them is quicker, preparing the bites in batches works best. If you stack them, you may have a few that are really soft and break apart when you try to flip them over.

Per serving: Calories: 165; Total fat: 6g; Saturated fat: 1g; Cholesterol: 3mg; Sodium: 233mg; Carbohydrates: 23g; Fiber: 2g; Protein: 6g

Homemade Cherry Breakfast Tarts, page 32

MEASUREMENT CONVERSIONS

Volume Equivalents (Liquid)

Standard	US Standard (ounces)	Metric (approximate)
2 tablespoons	1 fl. oz.	30 mL
¼ cup	2 fl. oz.	60 mL
½ cup	4 fl. oz.	120 mL
1 cup	8 fl. oz.	240 mL
1½ cups	12 fl. oz.	355 mL
2 cups or 1 pint	16 fl. oz.	475 mL
4 cups or 1 quart	32 fl. oz.	1 L
1 gallon	128 fl. oz.	4 L

Oven Temperatures

Fahrenheit (F)	Celsius (C) (approximate)
250°	120°
300°	150°
325°	165°
350°	180°
375°	190°
400°	200°
425°	220°
450°	230°

Volume Equivalents (Dry)

Standard	Metric (approximate)
⅛ teaspoon	0.5 mL
¼ teaspoon	1 mL
½ teaspoon	2 mL
¾ teaspoon	4 mL
1 teaspoon	5 mL
1 tablespoon	15 mL
¼ cup	59 mL
⅓ cup	79 mL
½ cup	118 mL
⅔ cup	156 mL
¾ cup	177 mL
1 cup	235 mL
2 cups or 1 pint	475 mL
3 cups	700 mL
4 cups or 1 quart	1 L

Weight Equivalents

Standard	Metric (approximate)
½ ounce	15 g
1 ounce	30 g
2 ounces	60 g
4 ounces	115 g
8 ounces	225 g
12 ounces	340 g
16 ounces or 1 pound	455 g

RECIPE INDEX

INDEX

ACKNOWLEDGMENTS

To my family: I love you and thank you for always believing in me and for allowing me to invade your kitchens every holiday.

To my close friends: Thank you for pushing me and reminding me of my drive and resilience.

To my loyal subscribers and everyone who has supported *Stay Snatched*: I am grateful for you all. Thanks for every email, social share, and comment. You keep me humble.

A special thank you to my friend Amber Bennett. You listened and encouraged me when my vision of becoming a blogger was a distant dream.

ABOUT THE AUTHOR

Brandi Crawford is a blogger and the creator of *Stay Snatched*, a blog that focuses on quick and easy, healthy recipes. After constant crash dieting and struggling to reach weight loss goals, she shifted her lifestyle focus and started to create her own recipes that are nutritious but do not compromise on flavor or taste. She also works full-time in a corporate space and understands the value of super easy recipes.

Stay Snatched has been featured in *Women's Health Magazine*, *Country Living Magazine*, *Shape Magazine*, *Essence*, and *Delish*, among other media outlets. "Stay snatched" is a term that defines a movement that encourages consistent focus on physical and mental health. With an engaged Instagram following at @Stay_Snatched, more than 300,000 monthly viewers to her blog, StaySnatched.com, and more than 4 million monthly viewers on Pinterest, she is recognized as a trusted resource for air fryer recipe development.

When she isn't in the kitchen, you can find her in the gym or chasing her 2-year-old Yorkshire terrier. She lives in Kansas City, Missouri.

CPSIA information can be obtained
at www.ICGtesting.com
Printed in the USA
LVHW022039301018
595367LV00029B/533/P

9 781641 520492